Operations Management in Hospitality Industry

Operations Management in Hospitality Industry

William Cage

Operations Management in Hospitality Industry
William Cage
ISBN: 978-1-63989-395-9 (Hardback)

© 2022 States Academic Press

Published by States Academic Press,
109 South 5th Street,
Brooklyn, NY 11249, USA

Cataloging-in-Publication Data

Operations management in hospitality industry / William Cage.
  p. cm.
Includes bibliographical references and index.
ISBN 978-1-63989-395-9
  1. Hospitality industry--Management. 2. Production management. 3. Operations research. I. Cage, William.
TX911.3.M27 O64 2022
647.950 68--dc23

This book contains information obtained from authentic and highly regarded sources. All chapters are published with permission under the Creative Commons Attribution Share Alike License or equivalent. A wide variety of references are listed. Permissions and sources are indicated; for detailed attributions, please refer to the permissions page. Reasonable efforts have been made to publish reliable data and information, but the authors, editors and publisher cannot assume any responsibility for the validity of all materials or the consequences of their use.

Trademark Notice: All trademarks used herein are the property of their respective owners. The use of any trademark in this text does not vest in the author or publisher any trademark ownership rights in such trademarks, nor does the use of such trademarks imply any affiliation with or endorsement of this book by such owners.

For more information regarding States Academic Press and its products, please visit the publisher's website www.statesacademicpress.com

Table of Contents

	Preface	**VII**
Chapter 1	**Front Office Operations: An Overview**	**1**
	a. Front Office	1
	b. How to become a Hotel Receptionist	2
	c. How to Work the Front Desk at a Hotel	13
	d. How to Answer the Phone at Work as a Hotel Receptionist	19
	e. How to write a Professional Email	23
	f. How to make Hotel Reservations for Student Groups	36
Chapter 2	**Customer Service Operations in the Hospitality Industry**	**40**
	a. How to give Great Customer Service using E-Mail	40
	b. How to Handle Customers	42
	c. How to Handle Angry Customers	53
	d. How to Deal with Rude Customers	58
	e. How to Deal with Aggressive Customers	66
	f. How to Handle Customer Complaints Quickly	73
	g. How to Handle Customer Complaints about Food	80
	h. How to develop a Relationship with a Customer	85
Chapter 3	**Service and Housekeeping Operations**	**93**
	a. How to Design a Hotel Room	93
	b. How to make a Hotel Bed	102
	c. How to Improve Service Quality at your Business	109
	d. How to set up a Commercial Kitchen	123
	e. How to Clean Drinking Glasses in Hotel Kitchen	128
	f. Housekeeping	132
	g. How to Organize a Laundry Room in Hotel	132
	h. How to Dry Clean in Hotel Laundry	136
	i. How to Wash Feather Pillows	141
	j. How to Wash Towels	147
	k. How to Clean a Sofa in Hotel	159
	l. How to Clean Fake Plants	168
	m. How to Clean Pots and Pans	176
Chapter 4	**Maintenance Operations: An Integrated Study**	**180**
	a. How to Maintain Swimming Pool	180
	b. How to take Care of a Pool	188
	c. How to Raise pH in Pool	195
	d. How to Eliminate and Prevent Green Algae in a Swimming Pool	200
	e. How to Vacuum Pool and Backwash the Filter	207
	f. How to Drain and Refill Swimming Pool	211
	g. How to Clean a Water Fountain	216
	h. How to Maintain Indoor Fountains	220
	i. How to Maintain Outdoor Fountains	224

Chapter 5	**Security Operations in Hotel**	**226**
	a. How to choose the Right Location for your Outdoor Security IP Camera	226
	b. How to Install a Security Camera System for a Hotel	229
	c. How to Replace a Smoke Detector	238

Permissions

Index

Preface

The hospitality industry is multifaceted and involves direct interaction with clients, customers and potential guests. Operations management in the hospitality industry involves careful planning of human resources, housekeeping operations, front desk management and food and beverages management. Efficiency and high quality of service are the targets that are to be kept in mind in this sector. Good operations management oversees all aspects of running a hotel from meeting clients to stocking and replenishing essential items. The topics covered in this extensive book deal with the core aspects of operations management in the hospitality industry. It will serve as a reference to a broad spectrum of readers.

To facilitate a deeper understanding of the contents of this book a short introduction of every chapter is written below:

Chapter 1- Front office operations in the hospitality industry deal with the reception of clients as well as guest registration, cashier work and message service. Complaints, queries and requests of clients are also received by those in-charge of front office operations. This chapter is an overview of the subject matter incorporating all the major aspects of front office operations.

Chapter 2- Customer loyalty is an important aspect of hospitality management. It is very important for people associated with the hospitality industry to provide services for every type of customer. A good impression can increase standing with the customer. The chapter strategically encompasses and incorporates the major components and key concepts of customer service operations, providing a complete understanding.

Chapter 3- Housekeeping operations ensure that indoors of a building such as a hotel is neat and tidy. Various service and housekeeping operations include making a bed, maintaining glassware, linens, pots and plants, etc. Service and housekeeping operations is best understood in confluence with the major topics listed in the following chapter.

Chapter 4- Outdoor maintenance operations in resorts, theme parks and hotels include pool management, fountain management, etc. Water in the swimming pool need to be filtered as well as treated chemically for eliminating waterborne diseases. The aspects elucidated in this chapter are of vital importance, and provide a better understanding of maintenance operations in the hospitality industry.

Chapter 5- Guests need to feel relaxed and comfortable and safety becomes a key aspect of hotel management. Security guards, video surveillance, smoke detectors, adequate lighting are important measures that can be taken to prevent harm to the guests. This chapter discusses the methods of hotel security operations in a critical manner providing key analysis to the subject matter.

I owe the completion of this book to the never-ending support of my family, who supported me throughout the project.

William Cage

Front Office Operations: An Overview

1

Front office operations in the hospitality industry deal with the reception of clients as well as guest registration, cashier work and message service. Complaints, queries and requests of clients are also received by those in-charge of front office operations. This chapter is an overview of the subject matter incorporating all the major aspects of front office operations.

Front Office

Front office at Jain University, Bangalore

The front office or reception is an area where visitors arrive and first encounter a staff at a place of business. Front office staff will deal with whatever question the visitor has, and put them in contact with a relevant person at the company. Broadly speaking, the front office includes roles that affect the revenues of the business. The term *front office* is in contrast to the term *back office* which refers to a company's operations, personnel, accounting, payroll and financial departments which do not interact directly with customers.

The front office receives information about the customers and will then pass this on to the relevant department within the company. The front office can also contact the marketing or sales department should the customers have questions. The company needs to give training to the front office manager as this position will come in contact with customers the most.

The most common work for the front office staff will be to get in touch with customers and help out internally in the office. Staff working at the front office can also deal with simple tasks, such as printing and typing tasks and sorting emails. Although front office staff might only need to perform tasks such as answering the phone, using the printer and fax machine, training is still needed on these tasks.

Front office is related to a service delivery system, where employees engage with customers. It uses the parameter of labor intensity to figure out the distinctive characteristics of a service.

Hotels

At hotels, *front office* refers to the front desk or reception area or the core operations department of the hotel. This would include the reception and front desk, as well as reservations, sales and marketing, housekeeping and concierge. This is the place where guests go when they arrive at the hotel. Employees working in the front office will confirm guest reservations and also attend to guest complaints and queries.

The employees who work in the lobby of the hotel are also part of the front office as they deal with guest directly. The concierge, cashier, porter, and mailing service are included in the front office.

Receptionist

Receptionists in Stockholm, Sweden

A receptionist is an employee taking an office or administrative support position. The work is usually performed in a waiting area such as a lobby or front office desk of an organization or business. The title *receptionist* is attributed to the person who is employed by an organization to receive or greet any visitors, patients, or clients and answer telephone calls. The term *front desk* is used in many hotels for an administrative department where a receptionist's duties also may include room reservations and assignment, guest registration, cashier work, credit checks, key control as well as mail and message service. Such receptionists are often called *front desk clerks*. Receptionists cover many areas of work to assist the businesses they work for, including setting appointments, filing, record keeping, and other office tasks.

How to become a Hotel Receptionist

The hotel receptionist's role is vital, as they are essentially the face of the organization, being customer-facing and in charge of booking reservations. Gaining office administration experience and maintaining a professional attitude can help you to land a job as a hotel receptionist. Take hospitality courses and learn a new language to impress future employers, and show potential bosses that you will provide excellent customer service by maintaining a network of contacts who can refer to your skills.

Part 1
Learning about the Role

1. Understand the job description. While job duties will vary from hotel to hotel, there are certain responsibilities that all hotel receptionists are required to manage. These include handling reservations and cancellations, processing payments, answering guests' questions, taking messages, and answering the phone.

- This role requires you to be able to stay calm during stressful situations. Practice both your patience and your negotiating skills.

2. Prepare to work a variety of shifts. Working as a hotel receptionist will require you to work days, nights, weekends, and sometimes overnight. Be prepared to keep a flexible schedule.

3. Get a well-balanced education. A minimum of a high school diploma will be required, and some

college courses or a degree in hospitality will also help you to become a hotel receptionist. Learning a second language, especially one used by tourists in the location that you wish to work in, can be advantageous.

- Take English and communications classes that will provide you with the ability to communicate effectively both verbally and in writing.

- Take math and finance classes so that you are prepared to handle payments and money.

- Look for opportunities to take hospitality courses. Many community colleges and online schools offer classes in travel, tourism, and hotel management.

Part 2

Gaining Experience

1. Obtain experience in office and front desk functions. Work as a receptionist or an office assistant in a professional setting. This will help you learn skills required of a hotel receptionist.

- Getting experience managing a front desk can make you a valuable candidate for hire. Remain on good terms with former employers so that they can provide you with a recommendation.

- Answer phones, greet customers, organize paper and computer files, and get experience managing multiple administrative functions.

- Maintain a network of contacts. Stay in contact with higher-ups and terminate your employment on good terms with your employer so that they can give you a personal reference when you ultimately apply to a hotel receptionist role.

2. Sharpen your customer service skills. Working as a clerk in a retail setting, or a call center will give you the customer service experience that you need to become a hotel receptionist.

- Provide answers to questions, resolve complaints, and maintain a cheerful, positive and professional attitude when dealing with customers.

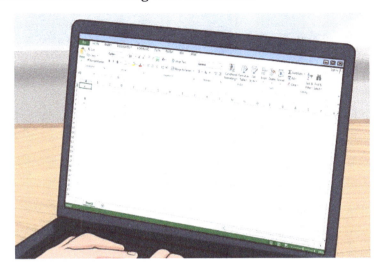

3. Learn various types of computer software. Stay up-to-date with technology, since you may need to learn new computer programs quickly. Many hotels will use specific databases and online reservation systems. Master a variety of programs so that you can be prepared for any software scenario.

- Learn how to use the Microsoft Office suite, including Word, Excel, Access and Outlook. Become familiar with creating a spreadsheet of data, as data entry will be a key part of your job.

4. Put together a resume that reflects your education and experience. Make sure that you have an objective section, which highlights your goal of becoming a hotel receptionist. Emphasize your strengths and any relevant skills. Use a sample resume to format the document correctly.

- Be sure to proofread your document for spelling errors and be sure to use professional language throughout.

Part 3
Finding a Job

1. Look for job opportunities. Check online job search websites such as CareerBuilder, Monster and Indeed. You can perform a search using specific keywords such as "hotel receptionist" and choosing the city or state you want to work in.

2. Call hotels in your area. Call the front desk and ask whether they are hiring a receptionist. You may instead want to visit in person so that employees will be able to connect your face with your name.

   - Drop off your resume at local hotels where you would like to work. Ask to speak to the manager and introduce yourself. This will give you a chance to demonstrate your professional and positive attitude.

3. Apply for the job. Once you find a job, send a resume and a cover letter to the hiring manager. Your cover letter should express why you are interested in the receptionist role, and which assets

you have that you would bring to the role. If you have previous experience working as an administrative assistant or receptionist, be sure to mention that in the cover letter.

- Keep your cover letter limited to one typed page, as the employer has to read through many applications. Use positive and energetic language to convey your personality throughout.

4. Interview for the role. Wear professional clothes, and take note of what their current receptionist wears in order to maintain a consistent look. Hotels value their branding, so if the hotel uses specific colors in their logo and branding, wear those colors to the interview. Be prepared to answer questions about your past experiences and your future goals with the company.

- Following the interview, send an email thanking the interviewer for taking the time to meet with you. Hopefully, you will hear back within a week or two with news that you got the job.

How to be a Good Receptionist

Every office that presents itself to the public in any way requires a face to meet the public. Although excellent communication over the phone and by email are important to the reception staff, it is the face-to-face communication that distinguishes a receptionist from a Customer Service Representative. Oftentimes, when a person (vendor, applicant, community member) enters your workplace, the first thing they will see is the receptionist- and first impressions are always important.

Part 1

Having the Right Skills

1. Have top-notch organizational skills. Receptionists are the people that represent the face of the

company--they are the ones that clients first speak with them and the people and coworkers go to for information and event planning. Aside from taking calls and directing visitors, they often deal with clients, organize events, set up meetings, etc. With all of these responsibilities, receptionists need to be really organized while dealing with multiple demands at once. A person won't last long as a receptionist if he or she can't juggle more than one thing at a time and deal with them in an orderly fashion.

- A great way to stay organized is to invest in a filing system that works best for you. It is important to know what papers and information your boss, your coworkers and your clients may need. Keep all of this information in separate folders--be they on your computer desktop or in hard copy. Organize your filing system in a way that works best for you--if that requires neon sticky notes attached to everything, so be it.

- Being organized also means being self-motivated--you don't need anyone else to tell you how to do something, or keep you on track. If you are organized, you will know what tasks you need to complete each day, and what tasks are priorities.

- Have phone numbers handy. (lots and lots) i.e. co-workers, employers, contractors, vendors, emergency contact numbers, etc. You will need them all at one point or another. Keep the phone numbers organized on a Rolodex or appropriate computer program.

2. Have some knowledge about technology under your belt. The number one piece of technology receptionists have to deal with is the telephone--and all of the buttons and separate lines that it comes with. Computer skills are also a must--most receptionists have to know how to use email and must be skilled at word processing. It is also helpful to know how to create spreadsheets, and use any industry-specific programs.

- Keep in mind that if the copier, scanner, or printer are near your desk, you will mostly likely be depended on to use them (and troubleshoot for coworkers who run into problems while using them.) Once you know the kind of machine being used at your office, brush up on its main functions and the ways to fix common problems.

Front Office Operations: An Overview | 9

3. Be dependable. A receptionist is counted on to man the desk at all times--it reflects poorly on the company if no one picks up the phone, or there is a line of people waiting to be helped. Make being dependable a priority--if your boss knows that you are reliable and are always there to help, you become indispensable.

4. Possess excellent listening skills. A big part of being a receptionist is listening to people--whether it is on the phone, a question a client is asking, or information being relayed to you. Being able to listen well will make you more efficient--you will be able to solve problems more quickly when you understand what the person is asking the first time around, and you'll connect clients to the person they are trying to reach quickly.

5. Take notes on everything. If a boss asks you to do something, takes notes on the specifics. If a customer calls, make sure to write down their information (name, contact information, what they

want, etc.) Notes are a great way to stay organized and remind you of all the little things that come up during the day. Keep your notes in a notepad and have it with you at all times. You will be surprised by how helpful they are, especially when trying to remember what the person who called five hours ago wanted.

- Make sure that you write out messages in detail and read over what you have written and most importantly when taking a message, repeat back the message and contact info that you were given so that you can make sure before you hang up that you have the proper information to relay.

6. Answer the phone politely with a standard greeting such as "Good Morning, Thank you for calling our company, my name is ___, how may I help you? Make sure the phone is answered on the first or second ring. It is not good to keep people on hold for more than one minute. (It's longer than you may think.)

- Listen carefully to the name of the person the caller is asking for. Repeat back to caller if necessary. Cell phones often distort sounds. Write the person's name to whom the call is directed if pronunciation is difficult.

- Direct the call politely with a standard phrase such as "One moment please for Mr. Smith." Or if that individual is on the phone, "I am sorry, Mr. Smith is on the phone at the moment. Would you like to wait on hold or would you like to leave him a voicemail message?" Politely thank them and direct the call accordingly.

7. Greet delivery personnel with the same professionalism and politeness as any other visitor. You may be required to sign for deliveries. Make sure your signature is legible. Delivery personnel may need directions where to leave packages. Make sure you contact appropriate employees for such matters.

8. Handle customers who come to your business with efficiency and politeness. After the visitors identify who they are and who they are looking for, contact that individual and let her/him know who is there. A standard appropriate phrase is "Mr. Smith, Mr. Jones from XYZ Corporation is here to see you for his 2 o'clock appointment." Always get a first and last name and the name of the organization they are from. It is helpful to ask if they have an appointment with Mr. Smith. Mr. Smith will give you instructions about where to have visitor wait and for how long. You can then tell visitor "Mr. Smith will be with you in a moment." or "Mr. Smith said that he is finishing up a meeting and will be with you in 5 minutes. You may have a seat. Thank you."

Part 2

Presenting yourself Well

1. Have a positive attitude. As mentioned above, receptionists are the face of a company--they are who clients deal with first, and the people who answer the questions of people who can't come into the office. No one wants to be greeted by a sour expression and a grumpy attitude. Make it a priority to always have a smile on your face and a cheerful, upbeat personality. Remember to stay patient with challenging customers, even if they get on your last nerve.

- Even you come up against a challenging client, remind yourself that you are a strong, happy individual. Tell yourself that they are acting out of frustration but know that as long as you are trying your best to accommodate them, you are not the one at fault. It is better to be the one that keeps your head than the one who explodes and looks like an ornery, mean person.

2. Have a greeting ready. Its always important to greet your clients in a friendly way. Even if you continue what you are doing before helping them, its important to greet them so that they feel acknowledged and know that you will help them in a moment.

- Some greetings are "Hi! Welcome to [Business name]" or "Good morning! If you'll have a seat, I will be with you in just a moment!"

3. Be courteous. Be respectful. Treat everyone like they are the most important person that has walked into the office that day. This is your job- nobody cares about how you got stuck in traffic this morning, how you ruined your brand new purse, or even how you lost your favorite CD. Leave personal matters at home. (Even if you don't respect their message or the way they convey it- fake it) Overall, make sure the person is totally relaxed and happy to talk to you.

4. Dress to impress. You are representing a business, thus you should dress the part. Invest in

some business casual clothes. Alternatively, if you are a receptionist at a specific sort of store (such as a clothing store) you may consider dressing the part by buying some of the store's clothing and wearing them. Tend to the conservative, unless you work somewhere where fashion, trendiness, or other factors are pushed to the forefront.

- Check to see if your business has a specific dress code. Your business may be fine with casual dress, just remember that you should never dress *too* casually (sweats should be banned from the workplace.)

How to Work the Front Desk at a Hotel

Working at a hotel in a remote destination or in your favorite city is a dream many people have and achieve. When you are working at a front desk in a hotel, interpersonal skills are crucial to succeeding. You must always greet guests with a smile, and try to anticipate their needs by being attentive. It is also very important that you know your hotel's safety protocols so you can handle stressful and/or threatening situations. Additionally, answering phone calls, taking reservations and assisting current guests are routine procedures that every desk clerk must do.

Method 1
Landing the Job

1. Search for job openings. Search the websites of hotels in your area for job openings. Make sure to search popular job listing sites as well, since many hotels use these systems to post openings. Additionally, contact your local chamber of commerce and tourism boards to find out when job fairs are being held for hotel positions.

- Plan on attending job fairs to find out about new positions, as well as insights on the industry. Do not forget to bring a polished resume to these events.

2. Submit an application and resume. You will most likely need to fill out an application and submit a resume, as well as a cover letter. Make sure to outline your education, work history, related experience and skills that pertain to the job, like customer service skills.

- You may be required to submit your materials online, or hand them in. If you hand them in, then make sure to dress professionally.

- If you have previous experience working at a hotel, try to obtain one or two letters of recommendation from your manager and supervisor.

3. Set up an interview. If your qualifications match the hotel's expectations, then you will receive a callback. The hotel manager will want to set up an interview with you before they offer you a job. Set up an interview time that is both convenient for you and the manager. Make sure to prepare for the interview before you go in.

- Common interview questions are "Can you tell me a little bit about yourself?" "What is your work style?" "Why are you interested in this job/organization?" "What is one of your proudest accomplishments?" "What can you do for us that other candidates cannot?"

- Since first impressions are very important, remember to dress professionally in business attire for the interview.

Method 2
Checking Guests in and out

1. Greet guests with a smile. Your face is the first thing hotel guests will see upon arriving, which makes you the ambassador for the hotel. So it is very important that you are smiling while working the front desk, especially when you greet guests. A genuine smile will help guests feel happy and welcomed about checking-in.

- To personalize the experience for your guests, refer to them by a title and their last name, for example, Mr. Smith.

2. Assess your guests and their needs. While you are checking guests in, ask them questions about their stay so you can anticipate any future needs. Additionally, use cues like body language to ensure that your guests have a comfortable stay while at the hotel.

- For example, ask your guests if their stay is for leisure or work. If it is for leisure, ask them if they would like any recommendations for dinner or things to do around the local area. If it is a work trip, then let them know where your conference rooms and computers are. Also, see if they need a wake-up call in the morning.

- If one of your guests has a baby, for example, make sure to offer additional services, like a crib or bottle warmers, to help them feel at home.

3. Make light conversation with your guests. Do this while you are checking them in. By conversing with your guests, you can help them feel welcome. Making meaningful conversation with your guests signals that you (and the hotel) genuinely care about them and their stay at the hotel.

- For example, ask them how their flight or drive went. If it did not go so well, then offer them a complimentary breakfast, lunch or dinner.

4. Enquire about your guests' stay. Make sure to do this when your guests are checking out. Ask them if their stay went well, especially if there were some issues with their stay. See if the hotel's solution met their expectations or not.

- If not, ask the guests what the hotel can do or work on to ensure a better experience, or direct them to fill out a survey.

Method 3

Dealing with Stressful Situations

1. Remain calm and confident. This is very important during stressful or busy situations, which are

most likely to occur during peak seasons. When faced with a stressful situation, take a couple deep breaths, smile and then proceed to help the guests. Smiling, standing straight and talking calmly will signal to your guests that you are equipped to handle the situation.

- Make sure to call for assistance if you cannot handle a situation on your own.

2. Employ safety measures. Make sure to check entrances and exits constantly for any potential threats to the hotel and the guests' safety. Additionally, staying visible throughout your shift can help deter unwanted guests and situations. If your hotel has security cameras, make sure to watch these constantly for suspicious activities.

- It is very important that you are familiar with your hotel's safety protocols. This way you can confidently manage dangerous situations like theft, break-ins, and robberies, as well as natural disasters and threats.

- Make sure you report injuries and other emergencies to the police.

3. Apologize for any inconveniences. Calm upset or explosive guests by taking responsibility for the problem or issue. Apologize on the hotel's behalf. When communicating with your guest about the issue, respond to your guest in a friendly, calm manner and remember to smile.

- For example, if your guest is upset about their room not being ready, apologize and offer them a complimentary drink or appetizer at the hotel's restaurant or bar while they wait for their room. You can also offer to hold their luggage for them while they wait.

Method 4
Completing Routine Procedures

1. Answer phones. As a front desk clerk, a large part of your responsibilities will be to answer phones. Make sure to start and end calls with a professional greeting like, "Hello, this is the Harroldton's front desk, my name is Josie, how may I help you?" and "Thank you for choosing Harroldton's."

2. Take reservations. When you are taking reservations, inform the guests about the types of rooms that the hotel offers. Also let the guests know about local restaurants, parks, and entertainment centers that are nearby. Do not forget to tell them about any additional accommodations that will enhance their stay. In addition to taking reservations, you may also need to cancel a reservation.

- If you have to cancel a reservation, ask the guest about their reasons for canceling. If the issue is with the hotel, apologize and see if you can resolve the issue.

3. Assist current guests. You will need to do this in addition to assisting arriving guests. Assisting

current guests consists of making courtesy calls and coordinating room and housekeeping services. You may also need to help guests with their luggage, assist them to their room, and inform them of the hotel's amenities.

How to Answer the Phone at Work as a Hotel Receptionist

Projecting a professional image at work is important for career success. Answering the telephone is something that almost every employee does, regardless of his or her position in the company. Answering the right way will project a positive tone, help the caller feel comfortable, and set you up to help answer whatever questions he or she may have.

Part 1

Picking up the Phone

1. Answer quickly. If you are in a hotel business, it is rude to keep people waiting. Get to the phone and answer before the third ring.

2. Put the phone up to your face. While you want to move quickly when answering the phone, you should be patient enough to actually get the mouthpiece to your face. Make sure you don't start talking until the phone is right up against you so that the person on the other end doesn't miss any information.

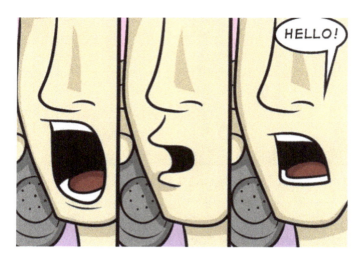

3. Take a deep breath before answering. Once the phone is up to your face, take a deep breath before giving your introduction. This will help you keep calm and controlled, making it easier to speak slowly and collect your thoughts.

4. Introduce your business and yourself. You want to make sure the other person on the line has called the right place and person, so make sure they know who you and your company are. Make sure you lead with the business name. You may want to give yourself a scripted greeting so that you don't have to think about what to say when the phone rings. This message will change slightly depending on your circumstances.

- If you are a Phone receptionist, it is important that you identify the whole company, as you are the caller's gateway to whatever they need. Something simple like "Hello, this is XYZ Enterprises, Nick speaking. How can I help you?" is good. This lets the caller know who you and your business are, and gives them an opening to continue talking.

- If you are part of an office, let the other person know what you do so they know what kinds of questions they can ask. Identifying yourself by saying "Hello, this is Jessica in Housekeeping" lets the other person know if they have reached the office or person they want, and if they should talk to someone else.

Front Office Operations: An Overview | 21

5. Keep a pen and notepad near the phone. This will let you jot down information quickly if the person want to leave a message or give you other information. You don't want to keep your caller waiting while you search for something to write with.

Part 2

Talking on the Phone

1. Smile as you speak. Even if you aren't in a good mood, putting a smile on your face and faking it can help you sound more pleasant to the person on the other end. It will probably help your mood a little bit as well.

2. Speak clearly and professionally. This is a professional setting, and it is important that both you and the other person understand each other clearly and precisely. Speak slowly and enunciate your words to make sure your information gets across.

- Avoid slang words like "Yep," "Sure," or "Nah." Instead speak with clear words like "Yes" and "No." You don't want any confusion between you and the caller over what either person said. Don't forget common polite phrases such as "Thank you" and "You're welcome" when appropriate.

- If you need to give someone specific numbers or letters, say passing along a name or phone number, it can be good to familiarize yourself with the phonetic alphabet. That way you can avoid confusion over letters that sound similar, like "B" and "V," with helpful hints like "V as in Victory."

3. Address the caller professionally. Use the person's title ("Mr. Jones") and not their first name, especially if you do not know the caller personally. Make sure you remember his name, and address him with it during the conversation.

- It may be helpful to write down the person's name after you get it in order to help you remember.

4. Transfer the person if necessary. If someone is calling you at work, he probably has a specific problem or issue he needs resolved. If you don't know how to answer a question or concern, don't try. Instead, offer to transfer him to someone who can help. This also shows that you are interested and willing to help solve your caller's problem.

- Many office phone systems will have a way to transfer calls. Make sure you know if your office does, and how it works. If not, get the right person's number, and pass that information to your caller.

- Be as polite as possible when doing this, and offer the transfer. Say something like "I'm afraid I can't answer that. Would you like me to transfer you to Brian, who can help you?" Make sure the person on the other end agrees before changing the call.

- If someone else isn't available, offer to take a message. Just remember to pass that message along.

5. End the call professionally. A clear and polite "Thank you" or "Good bye" lets the other person know that the conversation has finished and she can hang up. There shouldn't be any confusion over whether or not the conversation should continue.

- Let the other person hang up. She initiated the call, so you want to let her finish whatever she needed when she called in the first place. If you hang up when the caller isn't ready, it can appear rude, or you might miss important information.

How to write a Professional Email

Email is an important part of business communication, so it's critical to get it right. While emails aren't usually as formal as letters, they should still be professional and present a good image of you and your business, community, or position. Follow the steps in this tutorial to create business emails that are true to etiquette and ensure professionalism.

Part 1
Addressing the Email

1. Address your email. Type the email address of your recipient into the To field. Use the To field if you want to email contacts while encouraging their response.

- This field is for people that the message directly affects. If you are expecting someone to do something in reaction to your email, they should be in the To field.

- It's a good idea to include all of the people in your To field in the opening line of your email. This way, you engage everyone in the conversation from the start and inform everyone of who else is involved in the conversation.

- If you have included more than four people in the To field, address the group as a whole by starting your email with something like, "Hi Team, or "Good Morning All,"

- The To field can be used for as many addresses as you'd like. Remember, everyone who is directly involved and needs to take action should be included in the To field.

2. Use the Cc field (optional). The Cc (or Carbon Copy) field is used as a way to keep others "in the loop" without an obligation or requirement to reply or take action on the matter. Think of the Cc field as an FYI to distribute relevant information or updates to a number of associates who need only look through them. To add addresses to the Cc field, simply click on the Cc field and type as many addresses inside as you'd like.

- When Cc-ing multiple associates, each recipient will have access to the list of email Cc's.

3. Use the Bcc field (optional). The main purpose of the Bcc field is to send an email to a group of contacts that don't know each other. The Bcc field (Blind Carbon Copy) allows you to send a message to several contacts without them knowing who else got the message. To add addresses to the Bcc field, just click on the field and type in each email you need to include.

- Use the Bcc field to send an email to multiple associates who don't know each other. This protects the privacy of each recipient by keeping the list of recipients visible only to the sender and not to each recipient.

- Use the Bcc field when sending an e-mail to hundreds of people.

- Your contacts will be able to see anyone who the email was sent to in the To or Cc fields but not in the Bcc field.

4. Respond to an email Cc. If you are included in a Cc email, you are likely part of a handful of other associates all included in the conversation as well, and the sender may not be looking for or expecting a reply from any of you. If you do need to reply, think about the nature of your response and who it applies to. You can chose to "Reply to Sender" if you just have a note for the original writer of the email, or you can "Reply to All" only if the information is relevant to all involved in the conversation.

- Only when your comments are important to the entire group would you use the "Reply to All" field.

- Be careful when choosing to reply to all recipients on the email. You should avoid flooding other people's inboxes with irrelevant information whenever possible.

5. Respond to an email Bcc. If you have been included on an email Bcc you will only have the option to reply to the sender of the email and will be unable to see the list of other recipients who also received a Bcc. Simply click on the Reply button to compose an email to the sender.

6. Use a short and accurate subject header. Use as few words as possible to describe the topic or nature of your email. Try things like:

- "Leadership Meeting Update"
- "Issue Regarding Lunch Breaks"
- "Meeting Overview for March 12th"

Part 2

Composing the Email

1. Stick to a standard structure. When approaching a professional email, it's important to keep it clean, short, and clear. Say want needs to be said and keep it at that. You can develop your own structure that works best for you. Here is a basic structure to consider:

- Your greeting
- A pleasantry
- Your purpose
- A call to action
- A closing message
- Your signature

2. Write your greeting. To keep things professional and sophisticated, always open your email with a formal greeting, like "Dear Mr. Lu". Depending on your relationship with the recipient, you can address them as expected, either with their entire name and title, or just their first name.

- If your relationship is very casual, you can even say, "Hi Gabe".
- If you don't know the name of the recipient, you can use: "To whom it may concern" or "Dear Sir/Madam".
- If you are composing an email to a group of recipients who you have included in the To field and require a response from, greet them as a group (if the number of recipients is four or greater) or include each of their names in the greeting.
- If you are sending an email with Cc's, simply address the group as a whole if you have a great number of recipients, otherwise include each recipient's name in the greeting.
- If you are sending an email with BCC's, address the group as a whole by opening with something like, "Hi all".
- If you are emailing someone for the first time, keep introductions brief and let them know who you are in one sentence. For example: "It was great to meet you at [X event]."
- If you are not sure if an introduction is necessary and you've contacted the recipient before, but you're not sure if they remember you, you can leave your credentials in your email signature.

3. State the reason for your email. If you are initiating the line of communication, you are responsible for telling your recipients what the email is regarding. It is important to state your purpose

early. Business associates will want to be able to read your email quickly and get to the point. Take a minute to ask yourself why you are writing it and why you need your recipient to see it. This will help you avoid idle chitchat and cut right to the chase for a more professional email. This is also a good time to ask yourself: "Is this email really necessary?" Again, only sending emails that are absolutely necessary shows respect for the person you're emailing. Once you are ready to compose your email, try starting with something like:

- "I am writing to inquire about ..."
- "I am writing in reference to ..."
- "Please take the time to look over these changes and offer me your feedback..."

4. Thank the recipient (optional). If you are replying to a client's inquiry, or if someone has replied to one of your emails, you should begin with a line of thanks. For example:

- "Thank you for getting back to me..."
- "Thank you for your attention on this matter..."
- "Thank you for contacting Ocean Safari Scuba..."
- Thanking the reader is a great way to remain polite, professional, and on good terms with your recipient.

5. Keep the body of your email brief. With business emails, the less you include the better. Make each email you send out just about one thing. If you need to communicate about another project, compose another email.

- Try communicating everything you need to in just five sentences. Say everything you need to say, and no more. Sometimes it will be impossible to limit your email to just five sentences. Don't worry if you need to include more information.

- In the body of your email, include all relevant information and anything you may require from your recipients.

6. Include a call to action (optional). If you need your recipient to do something, don't just assume they will know what to do or when. Help them out by clearly outline what you need. Say something like:

- "Could you send me those files by Thursday?"

- "Could you write that up in the next two weeks?"

- "Please write to Thomas about this, and let me know when you've done so."

- Structuring your request as a question encourages a reply. You can say, "Let me know when you have done that."

7. Add your closing. To keep your emails professional, end your email with another thank you to your reader or a formal goodbye such as:

- "Thank you for your patience and cooperation"

- "Thank you for your consideration"

- "If you have any questions or concerns, don't hesitate to let me know"

- "I look forward to hearing from you".
- End your email with a proper closing before your name, like "Best regards" or "Sincerely"
- Avoid casual closings like "Cheers" unless you are good friends with the reader, as these types of closings are less professional.

8. Sign your name. In a professional email, your signature should include the following:

- Your name.
- Your job title.
- A link to your website.
- Links to social media accounts (optional).
- Necessary contact information.

Part 3
Sending the Email

1. Simplify your email if possible. Remember, your recipients are busy and they want to get to the meat of the email quick. Take a step back and evaluate your email. Here are some things to consider:

- Use short sentences, words, and paragraphs. This helps make the email quick and easy to read and understand.

- If it's possible to cut a word out, cut it out. Trim your sentences down to as short as possible.

2. Give your email a thorough proofreading. Professional emails require careful proofreading. Read your email aloud to yourself. This can help you catch a lot of spelling and grammar mistakes. Ask yourself:

- Is my email clear?

- Could my email be misunderstood?

- How would it sound if I were the recipient?

3. Keep it professional. You don't need to show your personality in your professional email. If you'd like, you can let it show subtly through your writing style, but stay away from emoticons, chat abbreviations (such as LOL), or colorful fonts and backgrounds.

- The only time it is appropriate to use emoticons or chat abbreviations is when you're mirroring the email language of the person you're writing to.

- Write like you speak. This can help you keep your email short, friendly, and personable.

- Don't say anything in an email that you wouldn't say to your recipient in person.

4. Send your email. Once you have proofread you email and have included all the necessary information and added each recipient to the appropriate field, click the send button.

Being an effective communicator is an asset in the workplace, and nowhere is this more true than when writing a formal email. With the way communication is evolving, however, it can sometimes be a challenge to strike the proper balance between polish and practicality in such an impersonal format. For work-related messages, it's always best to keep things terse, polite and to-the-point. Like any other form of correspondence, you'll want to begin with a friendly greeting, then lay out your message in short order and invite the desired response so that your recipient has a clear understanding of what action to take next.

Part 4

Crafting an Eye-Catching Introduction

1. Use the subject line wisely. Rather than filling the subject with one or two vague terms, let the recipient know up front what they can expect from your email. Otherwise, it might fail to make the impact that it's supposed to. Be as specific as possible when supplying a subject for the email without becoming overly wordy.

- "Upcoming Health Inspector Visit" is a stronger subject title than just "Health Inspector"
- When in doubt, think about what prompted the email in the first place and describe the situation in a few words.

2. Identify yourself right away. Stating your name and formal title or position will help the recipient tell who the message is from without the need for guesswork. This is especially important if

you're writing to someone you've never met. Even if your name is contained in your work email address, letting the other person know who you are is a common courtesy.

- Pique your recipient's interest by highlighting a common connection or shared experience ("We met at the annual Women as Leaders conference in Toronto last year").

- It's alright to skip the introduction if you're already acquainted with the person you're writing.

3. Specify whom you're writing to. The header of the email should consist of a brief but friendly greeting and the name of your recipient. In most cases, it's perfectly fine to open with a simple "Dear Marie." If the nature of your correspondence calls for something a little more formal, it's safest to use the recipient's name alone as the greeting to keep things short and sweet.

- If you're not on a first name basis with the person, stick with their last name to avoid potentially offending them.

- When you don't know your recipient's name, or it's unclear who might be answering the email, you can either open with "to whom it may concern" or simply substitute the name of the company.

- Keep in mind that most workplace emails are sent over public servers, and that other individuals may also be copied in your email. If privacy is a concern, you may wish to find a more discreet method of communication.

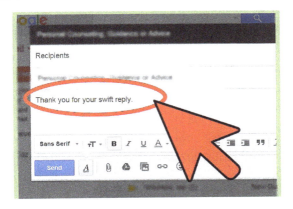

4. Thank the recipient briefly. Your reader is a busy person, so acknowledging them for taking the

time to read your email is a gracious gesture. Additionally, this will be your first opportunity to inform them of your reason for writing. "Thank you for considering my research grant proposal" sets a friendly tone while telling the recipient what they need to know.

- Beginning an email by expressing your appreciation also demonstrates respect, which can keep the message from coming across as cold or impersonal.

Part 5

Delivering your Message

1. Maintain a professional tone. When sending business emails, it's important to be especially mindful of the language you employ to avoid confusion or misinterpretation. In general, you shouldn't say anything in an email to your boss or coworkers that you wouldn't say to them in person. Your words should always be calm, polite and congenial, even in situations where you don't feel that way yourself.

- Once you've written your email, read it back to yourself to determine whether you've captured the right tone.

- Though it should go without saying, refrain from using any type of slang or profanity.

- While humor is often a valuable quality in the workplace, work-related emails are usually not the right vehicle for it.

2. Present the most important information first. As previously mentioned, you should assume that your recipient has a lot on their plate and make an effort not to take up too much of their time. After thanking them for their attention, get straight to the point. Don't mince words or feel the need to come up with an overly detailed introduction. Unlike more casual methods of correspondence, professional emails should be polite yet direct.

- Try an introductory sentence like "I'm writing to inform you that your membership has expired and needs to be renewed in person before you can continue receiving member benefits." You can then follow up with whatever pertinent details the recipient needs in order to take action.

- Most people tend to scan emails rather than reading each and every word. The nearer your main objective is to the beginning, the more likely your recipient is to pick up on it.

3. Keep the rest of the message concise. There's no sense in rambling aimlessly once you've stated your purpose. With the space you have remaining, provide any other details that you think are worth mentioning. Always use short, simple words and phrases to take as much of the work out of interpreting your meaning as possible.

- Observe the "five sentence rule"—messages shorter than five sentences may come off as brisk or rude, whereas anything longer than five sentences puts you in danger of losing your reader's attention.

- If for some reason you have to include a large amount of information, do it as a separate attachment.

4. Convey a clear idea or request. Once you've stated your reason for writing, articulate to your reader exactly how you'd like for them to respond. If there's something they need to know, tell them; if there's something they need to do, ask them. By the time they finish reading your message, your recipient should be ready to formulate a response.

- Experienced communicators refer to this as a "call to action," and it's a good way to ensure that your dialogue maintains a distinct sense of purpose.
- A call to action in a professional email might say something like "it's important that you memorize the security clearance number provided with this email" or "please update your summer availability by the end of the month."

5. Limit your email to a single topic. Confronting your recipient with too much information at once can leave them feeling overwhelmed. It's best to limit the scope of your email to one or two relevant subjects. Not only will this allow the reader to understand what's going on much faster, it will also help you keep your message succinct.

- Multiple topics or requests should be reserved for multiple emails.

Part 6

Wrapping Things up

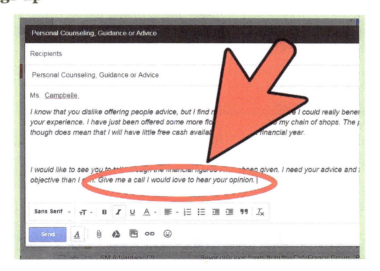

1. Tell the recipient how you expect them to follow up. Now that you've offered a call to action, give your reader a nudge in the right direction. A request to look over a financial report, for instance, might be accompanied by an entreaty like "let me know what you think of these numbers." That way, the other party won't be left wondering what to do with the information they've been given.

- Offering a definite time frame in which you'd like to hear back ("it would be ideal if we could have these documents organized before the meeting on Thursday") may ensure a swifter response.
- Try to reply to important emails within 24 hours.

2. Sign off with a custom signature. The signature at the bottom of the email should offer the recipient all the information they need about who you are so that there's no need to introduce yourself at length within the message. Be sure to include your full name, the name of your company, your title or position, your preferred email address and a phone number at which you can be reached directly.

- To save yourself some trouble, save your custom signature in whatever email platform you use so that it will be displayed automatically in future messages.

- Providing links to your social media accounts will give unfamiliar contacts a more complete picture of you.

- Don't bog down your signature with unnecessary details, quotes or graphics.

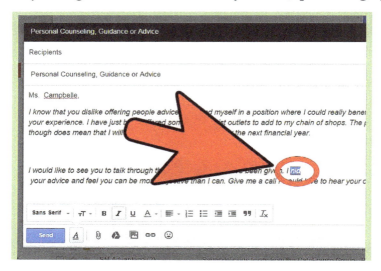

3. Proofread your email before sending it. Go back over your message thoroughly to make sure it's free of any typos, misspellings or unclear sentences. Careless mistakes can reflect poorly on you and the company you represent.

- Use your email platform's spell-checker feature to avoid accidental oversights.

- You can also take this time to make any last minute changes to the formatting that you think may make your email easier to digest.

How to make Hotel Reservations for Student Groups

When a group of students travel together, there are several details that need to be taken into consideration. There needs to be an adequate number of chaperones, and if it is an overnight trip, you will need to find a hotel that can accommodate a group your size. This can often be a challenge, especially if you are trying to book a hotel in a popular area during a busy season. Make hotel reservations for student groups by shopping around for good rates and booking well in advance of the trip.

Front Office Operations: An Overview | 37

Steps

1. Get an accurate number of travelers. Knowing how many students are going will have an impact on where you stay. Some hotels have limits to the number of rooms they will reserve for groups, or a maximum number of people who can take advantage of group discounts.

2. Set a budget. Determine how much can be spent per student or as a group before you make a reservation.

3. Shop around for a good deal. Check out a few hotels in the area you will be staying and compare rates.

- Call the hotels. Many people book hotels online, but when you are making a reservation for a group, it is better to speak to someone so you can explain your needs.

- Ask about group discounts. Many hotels offer a reduced rate when you book a group of rooms together.

- Find out if there are other perks available in addition to a group rate. These might include upgrades for chaperones or free movies and games in the rooms.

4. Choose the hotel you want to stay in. Once you have compared several hotels, pick one that can accommodate your student group and provide reasonable rates.

5. Give the hotel a deposit. Each hotel has different policies about how much of a deposit is required on group reservations.

- Find out when the balance will be due. You might need to pay in full when you check in, or at the time of check out.

6. Provide a list of student names to the hotel, if requested. This will help the hotel assign rooms to each guest. If you want to have certain students stay together, indicate how guests should be paired or grouped in the rooms.

- Note the names and contact information of the chaperones and other traveling adults.

7. Make sure appropriate restrictions are placed on charges that may be made to the rooms. Let the hotel know that the students in your group are not permitted to make phone calls, access the mini bar or take advantage of any other amenities you might want to restrict.

8. Gather as much information as you can from the hotel and share it with your student group.

- Ask students to pay attention to dress code, rules, emergency instructions and any other pertinent information in the hotel policies.

9. Be sure to thank the hotel after your stay if you had good service. Managing a large group of students can require extra attention from hotel management and staff.

- Let the hotel know you appreciate their good service by writing a positive online review or completing a survey card they provide.

Customer Service Operations in the Hospitality Industry

2

Customer loyalty is an important aspect of hospitality management. It is very important for people associated with the hospitality industry to provide services for every type of customer. A good impression can increase standing with the customer. The chapter strategically encompasses and incorporates the major components and key concepts of customer service operations, providing a complete understanding.

How to give Great Customer Service using E-Mail

The future of customer service is now. Technology has made seeking out support faster and easier than ever. But, has your digital age company sacrificed true service in the name of automation?

Today, finding customer support is as simple as writing an e-mail or picking up the phone. But, even though you're not face-to-face with your customers, you still leave a lasting impression. Do you come across as caring and competent, or menacing and mechanical?

Offering stand-out service on the Internet isn't as hard as it is rare. A good customer service representative will still put "service" first, even if they aren't face-to-face with the customer.

Steps

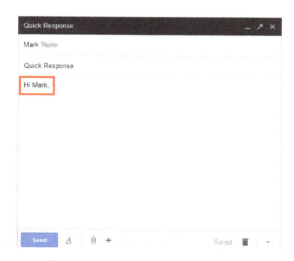

1. Give each customer a personal response. When a customer sits down to e-mail your company, it's because he needs help. He chooses e-mail because it's quick, but his request still warrants a satisfying and personal response! Companies eager to save time and money often take automation too far in their customer support. Each customer has a unique question, and deserves a unique answer. Even if you save time by copying and pasting stock replies, change the opening and closing to make the message sound less robotic.

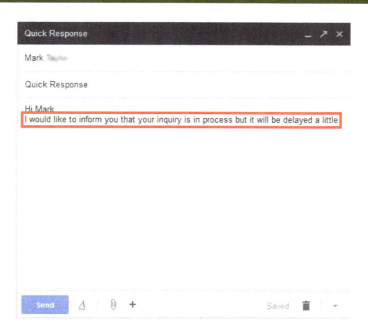

2. Be clear but sincere. When responding to customers' e-mail, be sincere and to the point. Before sending a message, try turning the tables. Ask yourself, "Would this answer satisfy me if I were the customer?" Take that extra moment to give your customer the help he deserves. It might mean the difference between a satisfied customer and a credit card chargeback.

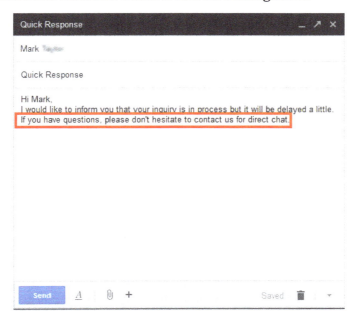

3. Offer live customer support. E-mail has become an acceptable form of communication. But, live customer support is still necessary. The plethora of information available online can be overwhelming to customers, especially those new to the Internet! Single your company out from the crowd by providing customers with a real person to talk to. Live phone support is an invaluable way to foster trust. When your customer has reached the end of his Internet rope, and just needs help, your toll free number is the answer he's looking for.

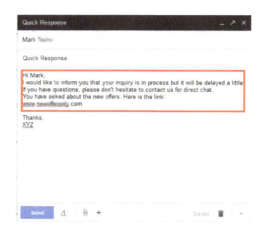

4. Make sure your support reps have all the answers. The presence of phone support will do no good if your staff doesn't know your product! Customer support reps should be warm and friendly, and willing to help with any aspect of your product. What a good feeling it is to talk to someone who feels confident in his product. It's even better if he's knowledgeable enough to solve your problem without transferring you all around the company.

How to Handle Customers

Anyone who's ever held a job working with customers knows how difficult it can be to stay calm and keep everybody satisfied day in and day out. Customer complaints, complex or unusual requests, and managers who only seem to be around when you're messing something up – it's a recipe for a meltdown if you aren't prepared. Read this guide to learn how to handle every customer with grace and confidence.

Method 1
Developing Good Service Habits

1. Take pride in your ability. Employers often talk about taking pride in your *work*, but a service worker's work isn't all that exciting, per se. Instead, take pride in your own ability to *do* that work. Start being impressed with how well you manage during each shift. There's no better way to encourage yourself to do even better than to let yourself believe that you're capable of doing better.

- In lower-level service jobs especially, you may not be treated as though you have much personal ability, but that's simply not the case. It takes poise, perseverance, and social skills to handle customers, even at a fast food drive-through window.

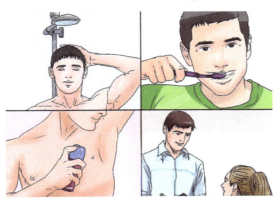

2. Put your best foot forward. The best way to handle customers is to never give them a chance to dislike you. A big part of that is making a positive physical impression on them. Dress neatly, in clean clothes. Bathe regularly, and brush your teeth and use deodorant every day. Walk with an easy stride, make eye contact, and speak in a loud, clear, relaxed voice. Your customers will feel as though they're in the hands of a professional right away, discouraging any urge to nitpick the rest of your performance.

- If you sweat a lot or have any other condition that might make you smell or look less than your best after a few hours on the clock, see if there's any way to bring some emergency hygiene supplies to work and pop out for five minutes partway through your shift to replenish.

3. Start with a smile. If you're really leaving your own worries, fears, annoyances, and insecurities at home each day, it's an easy next step to teach yourself to smile and be genuinely glad to greet every new customer. Don't be self-conscious — let your face open into the biggest, sunniest smile you've got every time you greet someone at work (even if it's over the phone, since a real smile comes through in your voice, too). You might be surprised just how much of a difference it makes in the way customers treat you.

- Don't forget to smile at your coworkers and, yes, even your bosses. It costs nothing except a little self-consciousness, and it will reduce your workplace stress considerably if you can keep it up. Smiles are contagious.

- Pay attention the next time you go out shopping or visit a restaurant, and you'll see that some service workers always seem sullen and vaguely resentful. That's because they aren't focused enough on the work, and are too concerned with who's "okay" to interact with and who's "not okay." Think about how unwelcome such people make you feel, and resolve not to make others feel that way at your own job.

4. Leave your "self" at home. This is one of the most important skills a customer service worker can learn, as it's often what separates the happy workers from the miserable ones. In a nutshell, you aren't at work to demonstrate who you are. You're only at work to do a good job and get paid. The customers who interact with you at your job don't know what pet peeves you have, what your favorite food is, or what you think of the clothes they're wearing – and just as importantly, *they don't care*. They're talking to you because they need service. Always keep that in mind.

- If you're insecure or nervous about what people think of you, leaving your worries at home should help you to deal more confidently with customers. Focus on their needs and wants instead of their thoughts about you. They aren't a part of your personal life, so it's safe to disregard what they might think of you.

- If you're constantly frustrated by customers or find yourself silently judging them (even the nice ones), leaving that bad attitude at home will help you relax and do your job more efficiently. Remember, the customers are the lifeblood of the business, and therefore of your paycheck.

5. Don't take things personally. Customers don't really have much invested in what they say about you; they're just reacting in the heat of the moment, for better or worse. Obviously, praise is prefer-

able to criticism, but either way, the customer's opinions don't matter as much as their continued business does. Just let everything they say slide over you and disappear. Continue providing the best service you can to each customer, regardless of how they react.

- Never take out a bad experience with one customer on the next customer you come into contact with. Compartmentalize the incident and see it for what it was – unpleasant, but isolated. Once you grasp that, it becomes easy to ignore. The only time a bad customer experience snowballs is when you take their bile and spread it around. By not taking your customers personally, you can be sure the buck stops with you.

- Be proud when you receive a compliment. However, don't take it as a cue to stop striving to provide even better service. The people who receive the most positive feedback from their customers are the people who never stop going the extra mile to make them feel happy and at ease.

6. Take your customers seriously. Many a young or inexperienced service employee has gotten chewed out by a manager (or even fired) for scoffing at a bizarre or rude customer request. The fact is, you should always, always, always assume the customer is serious. Customers very rarely kid, and there's no way to know what's going through their minds as they speak to you. Be pleasant and earnest when you respond, no matter how their words sounded to you.

- Remember, especially in brick-and-mortar service jobs, you'll sometimes run into customers with mental illness, developmental disabilities, or speech impediments. If you make a habit of always taking every customer request seriously, you won't put yourself in the awkward position of being rude to someone for something they actually couldn't help.

- Sometimes, customers are trying to have a joke at your expense. That's fine; it's no fun for you, but remember, it doesn't matter and won't make any difference in your life later. Keep in mind the steps you've read and stay separated from the experience. Don't take it personally.

    o Very often, if you approach a "joke" request as though it's serious, you can make the joke fall flat and steal a bit of the rude customer's thunder without being rude at all. The customer was probably assuming you weren't dedicated enough to really "fall for it;" once he or she sees that you were actually ready to do whatever you could to satisfy the request, his or her opinion of you will change for the better.

7. Be humble. A humble worker embodies all the qualities outlined above. She provides consistent service regardless of the customer or the customer's attitude, smiles and tries to get along with everyone who crosses her path, and doesn't let personal misgivings or rough transactions color her actions. A humble service employee also knows when to pass the torch to a manager. There are times when you can't satisfy a customer, or can't fill a special request. That's what managers are for. There's no shame in calling them to help.

- Don't seem frustrated or angry when you have to bring a manager over to sort things out for your customers; instead, frame it to them as an extra step you're glad to take to make sure they're satisfied. Customers want to feel glad that you're working for their benefit, not guilty or upset because their request bothered you.

- Once the transaction is finished, ask the manager (after the customer has gone) to explain what they did, and what you should do the next time a similar situation comes up. Sometimes you can learn new and useful information so you can provide a smoother customer experience next time.

8. Don't rush customers. You should always be in a rush to help them, but they can take all the time they need. If a line or queue is building behind an exceptionally slow customer, see if you can get someone else to take a part of the line for you.

- If nobody else can help, continue to smile and be pleasant. The customers know it's not your fault that things are held up; they might not be so forgiving if you seem to be slowing things down even more by losing your cool and making mistakes.

Method 2
Problem Customers and Customer Complaints

1. Learn more than just the rules. Most service businesses have a clear set of rules for their workers. However, there's almost always a second, more flexible set of "rules" that govern the lengths to which you can bend or break the posted rules in order to keep a customer satisfied. Knowing these will help you go above and beyond the call of duty (which more often than not, calms customers down regardless of the eventual outcome) without getting in trouble.

- Most often, only management is allowed to make these exceptions, but ask and learn all you can to find any customer situation where you're also allowed to bend the rules. Sometimes, mollifying an irate customer is just a matter of showing them you'll make an exception in their case. Learn how to do it safely.

2. Skip a beat. Sometimes, customers drop all pretense of politeness and say something rude or mean. Nine times out of ten, if you let it slide without even acknowledging that it was said, the customer will immediately feel guilty about crossing that line and become much more peaceful for the rest of the conversation.

- If you can directly respond to an insult as though you didn't even realize it was *meant* as an insult, that's even better. The customer will be on his or her best behavior for the rest of the transaction in most cases, because he or she has been given a free do-over on a needless insult and would like you to not figure out what the original intent of it was.

3. Kill them with kindness. This doesn't mean being passive-aggressive; it means responding to irate customers the same way you'd respond to your favorite customers. Many customers who heckle you are only trying to get a rise out of you so they have even more to complain about. Don't give them the satisfaction. Just keep providing service with a smile and a can-do attitude, at least until the customer crosses the line and begins to actually abuse you verbally. (At that point, more drastic measures may be required.)

- It's perfectly fine to gripe about customers, but do it well away from where other customers can hear you, and do it after they've left. If you don't have a good place to commiserate with your coworkers about a bad customer, you're better off just keeping it to yourself and venting at home.

4. Talk to management. When there's a recurring problem customer, it's up to your store's management team to set a policy for dealing with him or her. Let them know there's a customer who's become a real problem for you and your fellow workers, and ask for advice on what to do about it. In some cases, the problem customer will be removed from the store; in many, the manager will assume the responsibility of catering to the customer.

5. Know your limits. "The customer is always right" is a guideline for service, not a decree allowing customers to walk all over you. Doing everything you can reasonably do to make your customers happy is very different from enduring humiliation and abuse in the name of your job. While it's important to have a thick skin and not let most things upset you, once in a while, a customer will blatantly cross the line. At such times, you have the right to calmly ask them to stop, and explain how it makes you feel.

- Sadly, your freedom to put the kibosh on customer abuse varies somewhat from company to company. However, generally speaking, you're allowed to draw the line at being personally attacked, shamed or ridiculed in front of an audience, or physically assaulted.

- If the customer still won't stop attacking you, get help from your fellow employees. You always have the right to handle the customer with the assistance of a manager or coworker who's willing to assume the burden.

6. Stand your ground. Very, very rarely, a customer may decide to spend his or her day ruining your day for no good reason, and you'll find yourself without a manager or helpful coworker in sight. At these times, you need to look out for yourself first. Don't tempt the customer to lash out at you by showing your emotions, but don't stand for abuse, either. Tell the customer to wait while you get a manager; if they don't want a manager, tell them there's nothing more you can do for them, and that they need to leave. Look them in the eye and don't back down from what you're saying.

- Again, staying calm and collected is the most important thing in this situation. Don't raise your voice or say anything rude, and don't sob or cry. Don't even let yourself smile or frown. Any sign of uncontrolled emotion will either make the customer even angrier, or spur them to continue abusing you.

- Don't ask them to leave, tell them they *need* to leave. You can explain yourself, but don't waver. If you're suffering an extraordinary amount of customer abuse and there's nobody around to help you deal with it, it's better to get written up than it is to let your spirit be crushed. A decent employer won't fire you for acting in your own best interests in such an extreme situation.

Method 3
Fostering a Positive Coworker Environment

1. Understand why coworkers are important to you. Having coworkers on your side confers a wealth of benefits. When you get along with your coworkers, you have people at your level who can empathize with your day-to-day experience, which helps keep your stress level down on the job. Coworkers who like you are also easier to ask favors of, and more likely to provide favors for you without being asked. Finally, coworkers can give you advance warning about management changes, upcoming reviews, and anything you're doing or not doing that might result in disciplinary action.

- Experienced customer service veterans often say that any customer service job is bearable, and can even be enjoyable, as long as you and your coworkers like each other. Feeling as though you're a valued part of the team drastically increases your job satisfaction.

2. Treat coworkers similarly to customers. In particular, smile and say hello to every one of them, even if you don't like them or care about them, and even if they don't smile back. People are awash with insecurities, but nearly everybody appreciates a person who seems to like them enough to smile at them without trying to hide it.

- You should also follow the rule of leaving your "self" at home when interacting with co-workers. Don't get emotional with them. Keep conversations light and inconsequential.

- Don't assume your coworkers agree with your opinions. Instead, ask them what they think of something, so you can respond with your opinion in a way that won't offend or alienate them.

3. Be outgoing. Even if you aren't much for socializing, fake it at work. Once you've settled into your job, invite your fellow shift workers to come have coffee or a beer with you after ward – and keep doing it every week until people start to say yes. Agree to spend time at other people's functions, if they invite you. (If they don't, try not to sweat it – it's probably nothing personal against you.) Make conversation with coworkers whenever you share a break or have some down time.

- There's no call to put pressure on people to spend more time with you. Sometimes, your coworkers won't be interested. That's fine – again, don't take it personally. Ease off the social invitations if someone keeps refusing them; reduce your small talk to a simple "hello" if someone seems intent on having a quiet break instead of chatting with you.

4. Work hard. At the end of the day, the best way to endear yourself to your fellow workers is to be a good employee. Find things to do when there's downtime, to reduce the burden on your coworkers later. If you can, always be ready to go out of your way to assist your coworkers with whatever they need to get done. Don't wait to be asked; offer your help instead. Ask more experienced coworkers how they do things so well or so fast, and then take their advice to heart – everybody loves feeling respected for their practical skills and knowledge.

5. Don't gossip. There's no need to tell other people not to gossip (as it only upsets them), but don't do it yourself. In particular, when you feel the need to talk about someone else and they aren't around, speak as though they could walk over and hear you at any moment. Maintain neutrality when one person complains to you about someone else by saying things like "I don't know, I don't mind working with him/her." You can sympathize with other people's problems, but don't make them your own.

- If you have interesting or useful information about a coworker that you want to share, that's fine as long as you leave judgments and negative emotions out of it. State what you know, and let others fill in their own emotional response.

6. Communicate clearly. There's more to getting along with your coworkers than just being nice. You also need to be able to address issues calmly and clearly as soon as they arise. Your fellow employees already know you as someone who smiles at them and seems happy to speak with them; now let them know that you can't be walked across just because you're friendly. If a coworker is taking credit for your work, obstructing an important walkway, or otherwise disrupting the flow of your job, tell them immediately.

- Again, leave emotions out of the equation. Explain yourself clearly and coolly. For example, "I've seen you ring up a few of my customers without asking them who helped them, and it's costing me money. I always ask my customers who helped them, and I give commission credit to whoever they say. All I ask is that you do the same for me."

- In some cases, you may not be comfortable speaking to a coworker about such matters. It's fine to go through managerial channels to resolve these situations. Just remember that if you feel safe doing so, speaking to your coworker directly will often be seen by that coworker as more upstanding and honest on your part, since you aren't alerting management to the issue before giving him or her a chance to resolve it.

How to Handle Angry Customers

Handling angry customers can be one of the most challenging aspects of a job. Whether they confront you face-to-face, or you speak with them over the phone, chances are you are going to be met with frustration, aggressive anger, and little patience. The key to successfully managing an angry customer is to remain calm. Scroll down to Step 1 for tips on how to handle those angry customers.

Part 1

Understanding the Customer's Complaint

1. Remain calm and adjust your mindset. No one likes to get confronted by a yelling, heated person in a public space. However, your job in this situation is to stay cool and collected. While you may have the urge to yell right back at them, fight the urge! Yelling and getting angry will only escalate the situation. Instead, put on your best customer service attitude and buckle down--it's time to get to work.

- Never use sarcasm or obviously faked politeness. Behaving in such a way will only fuel the customer's rage and will make the situation a whole lot worse.

2. Listen actively to what the customer is saying. An angry customer generally just wants someone to

vent their anger to and today, you are that person. That means that you need to do your best to listen carefully to what they are saying. Give the customer your undivided attention--do not look around, space out or let other things distract you. Look at the speaker and really listen to what they are saying.

- When you listen to them, listen for the answers to these questions: What happened to make them upset? What do they want? What can you do to help?

3. Separate your feelings from the situation. If the customer is particularly angry, he or she may say something (or several things) that are really rude. Keep in mind that you should not take it personally--he or she is upset with the business, the product, or the service they have been provided with--they are not upset with you as a person. You will have to set your personal feelings aside.

- Keep in mind though, that if the customer becomes too abusive, or seems really threatening, you should tell them that you will go get your supervisor or someone else to help you resolve this problem. When you are walking back to the customer, fill your supervisor or helper in on the situation and explain why you felt you needed to come get them (ie. you felt really threatened, etc.) If worse comes to worse, you will have to ask the customer to leave. Know your organizations policy on when to call the authorities and how to document any encounter like this where noting specific details might be necessary for follow up.

4. Repeat the customer's concerns. Once the customer is done venting, make sure you know exactly what it is they are upset about. If you are still feeling a little unclear, repeat what you think the customer is upset about, or ask him questions. Repeating the problem back to the customer will show him that you were listening, and will also let you confirm the problem that needs to be fixed.

- A good way to make sure that you know exactly what the problem is, is to use calm and collected wording like "I understand that you are upset, and rightly so, that the pizza was delivered an hour late to your house."

5. Actively sympathize. Showing empathy will help make the customer understand that you really are trying to help them. Once you have confirmed what the problem is, show them that you feel really bad about it, and completely understand why they are upset. Say something like:

- "I completely understand your frustration--waiting for a pizza, especially when you're really hungry, is a horrible feeling."

- "You are right to be annoyed--delivery delays can throw off all whole night of plans."

6. Apologize. Let the customer know that you are genuinely sorry that this happened to them--regardless of whether or not you think they are being a bit dramatic about the situation. Along with empathizing, apologizing can go a long way. Sometimes upset customers just want to have someone apologize to them for the bad service. Hopefully the customer will cool down a bit once you apologize on behalf of the company.

- Say something like, "I am so sorry your pizza was not delivered on time. It's incredibly frustrating when that happens and I completely understand why you are annoyed. Let's see what we can do to make this right."

7. Call your manager over if the customer asks you to. If you are in the process of handling a situation and the customer demands that you call your manager or supervisor over, it is best to follow the wishes of the customer. However, if you can avoid having to get your manager involved, do it. Handling a situation on your own will show your supervisor that you have the wherewithal to deal with angry customers in a calm and collected manner.

Part 2
Moving Forward

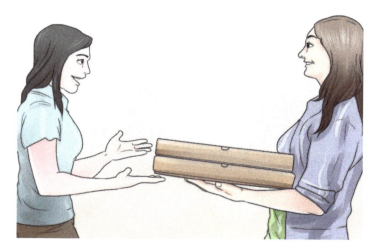

1. Offer a possible solution (or solutions). Now that you have heard what the customer is upset about, you should come up with a solution to provide them with. If you feel like you know a solution that will make your customer happy, then present it to her.

- For instance, in the situation with the late pizza, you might present something like, "I totally understand that you are upset your pizza was delivered late. I would like to refund your order and offer you a voucher for a free pizza. I will personally make sure that your next pizza gets delivered to you with the utmost haste."

2. Ask the customer for feedback. If you are not completely sure what would make your customer happy, then simply ask her. What would she like to have be done about the problem? Is there an outcome that would make her satisfied? Say something like:

- "What would you like to have happen? If it is within my power, I will see that it gets done."

3. Take action immediately. Tell your customer what you will do next to ensure that the problem is resolved. Give her your contact information, particularly if you are speaking with her over the phone, so that she can contact you if the problem arises again.

4. Take several minutes to yourself after the ordeal. Once your customer has left or you have hung up with her, take a few minutes to process what just happened and allow yourself to calm down.

Even if the customer left happily, these sort of situations can be really stressful. Take a few moments to destress and clear your mind. Documenting what happened is recommended- date, time, place, the events, and how it was resolved.

5. Follow up with the customer. Give your customer a call once the problem has been resolved. Ask him if everything is going smoothly. When you can, go the extra mile by sending a handwritten apology or by giving him a discount on his next purchase.

How to Deal with Rude Customers

Sometimes customers lose patience with the employee, some customers get frustrated with situational inconveniences, and some customers are just simply rude. Whether the customer's behavior was warranted or not, it can be incredibly stressful for employees to deal with rude behavior from customers. Knowing how to defuse a tense situation with a rude customer can help you feel happier and more comfortable at work, regardless of your profession.

Part 1
Holding Back your Emotions

1. Remain calm. The number one rule of customer service is to never lose your temper with a customer, no matter how rude he is being. Losing your temper with the customer will only escalate the situation, and could quickly result in your termination.

- Take a deep breath, drawing air in and out from your diaphragm instead of your chest. Deep breaths taken from the stomach help relax the body, even during stressful situations.

- Imagine something relaxing. It can be a place you've been or an entirely imaginary situation, but visualizing someplace or something that helps you relax can calm your racing thoughts and help you remain calm.

2. Don't take insults personally. This can be tricky for some people, especially those who tend to internalize criticism. The key is to remember that no matter what the customer is actually saying, the real cause of his problem has nothing to do with you as a person. He is most likely upset about the product he's purchased or the service he expected. It's entirely possible that the customer had unreasonable expectations to begin with, or perhaps there was a simple error made that has momentarily upset him. Focus on resolving the issue, rather than focusing on feeling hurt or insulted.

- Repeat a calming mantra to yourself internally. Something that will help center you and keep you calm would be key. Try thinking to yourself, "This is not my fault. He isn't mad at me, and it's not about me." It can help remind you that you haven't necessarily done anything wrong, and that the customer's temper will eventually pass.

3. Listen and learn what the real issue is. If a customer is being rude to you, it's possible that you or a coworker made a mistake. Or perhaps the customer did not get something he was supposed to get. Whether or not the customer's behavior is appropriate to the situation, the key is to listen

and try to understand what that actual situation is. It can be difficult to listen to an irate customer screaming obscenities at you, but beneath all that anger there is a problem that, most likely, you or a coworker can resolve. Tune out the customer's bad attitude, and zero in on the problem that is causing his bad behavior.

- Rather than making statements about the issue, stick to asking questions. This shows the customer that you're not being resistant to his complaint, and in answering your questions he may come to realize that there has been some sort of misunderstanding.

- Try to ignore whatever insulting or rude things the customer is saying, and focus on what his actual complaint is. If he isn't making his complaint clear, ask him politely but firmly, "Sir, I'm not following what the issue is. What can I do to help you today?"

- Try asking something like, "What were your expectations?" and follow that question with a polite "Why did you have those expectations?" This should be done carefully, as asking these questions without a calm and polite tone could come across as flippant. But these questions may help get to the root of the problem - for example, perhaps the customer misread an advertisement, or misunderstood what was being offered.

- You may need to state the reason for your stance on the issue. This is fine, but make sure you stick to the issue and your reasoning without attacking the customer or his logic. Calling his logic or his character into question will only escalate the situation and make him more difficult to deal with.

4. Speak low and slow. If a customer is getting increasingly irate, try lowering your voice and talking slower. This can have a somewhat soothing effect, and it also communicates to the customer that you are being firm and professional. It's important to consciously monitor your own tone and volume, because if you let yourself grow irate back at the customer it will only make things worse.

- If your correspondence with the customer is by email, take a few moments to center yourself before responding to the email. Take a few deep breaths, focus on something that makes you happy, and compose the email only after you've composed yourself.

Part 2
Assessing the Situation

1. Empathize with the customer. It may be difficult to empathize with someone who is being rude or even aggressive, but this is the best tactic. This shows the customer that you're not trying to ruin his experience, and lets him know that you're willing to work with him to resolve the issue. This can help defuse the undoubtedly tense situation between you and the customer.

- Let the customer know that you understand how he feels, and why he is upset. Try saying something like, "I understand why you're upset, sir. That sounds like a very frustrating situation."

2. Put yourself in the customer's shoes. Though you don't actually have to imagine the situation from the customer's point of view, it can be helpful. At the very least you should verbally summarize the situation to the customer, speaking from his point of view, to show the customer that you are on his side.

- Say something like, "Okay, sir, just to make sure I understand..." and then reiterate what the customer has told you. This subtly communicates to the customer that you trust his version of events, and that you take whatever happened very seriously.

3. Apologize politely to the customer. Once you've ascertained what the customer is actually upset about and recapped the situation with him, offer him a polite apology. It doesn't matter if you feel the customer deserves an apology. The reality of the situation is that you will not be able to defuse the situation without apologizing and making some effort at remedying the situation.

- Try saying something like, "I do apologize for that inconvenience, sir. Let me see what we can do to take care of that issue for you."

4. Don't back down. If the customer is wrong and he is being unreasonable, you should still apologize for any inconvenience, but you may need to hold your own ground to prevent the customer from walking all over you.

- Use firm but polite phrases, such as "Please let me finish," "That was not my question," or "That's not what I said."

- If you're communicating by email and the customer ignores something you've already said, try saying it again, or say something firm but polite like "Sir, I've already addressed that issue for you. Is there anything else I can do to help you today?"

5. Admit if there's nothing you can do. An irate customer will most likely continue to act out for as long as he thinks his behavior will change the outcome. If there's nothing that you or your co-workers can do, let the customer know. Be polite but firm - say something like, "I understand your frustration, and I'm terribly sorry, but there is nothing we can do about the problem." He may get more upset, but he'll most likely recognize he's defeated and leave after he feels he's said his piece.

Part 3
Resolving the Issue

1. If there is a simple solution, take it. If you are authorized to give customers a refund or exchange on an unsatisfactory product, do so. This will make the customer happy, and it will reduce your potential stress. Often times the simplest solution is the most desirable solution for everyone involved.

- You may want to consider asking the customer what he would like you to do to fix the issue at hand. Be aware, though, that if the customer is still ill-tempered or unreasonable, he may not be willing to offer a reasonable, practical solution.

2. **Look for written statements.** If the customer has an issue about a purchase, ask to see his receipt. Or if the customer is making demands that go against an agreement he signed, you can show him the agreement. No matter what the situation is, having some sort of documentation or supporting evidence can help you quickly shut down an irate customer's demands, if he's being unreasonable.

- If your correspondence with the customer is through a series of emails, you can email him proof of a contract or agreement, or simply refer him to an earlier email, if any previous correspondence dealt with the issue at hand.

3. **Consult with a manager.** If you are not authorized to give refunds or exchanges, or if you're certain that doing so would go against your company's policy in this instance, talk to your supervisor. You should also let a supervisor know if a customer becomes irate or unreasonable, as the manager may need to intercede before things escalate.

- Let your supervisor know what the customer's complaints are, what the issue seems to be caused by, and mention that the customer was being difficult.

- Your supervisor may give you instructions on how to proceed, or she may offer to step in and talk to the customer herself. At the very least, your supervisor should be able to help you strategize a reasonable solution to the problem, ideally one that would satisfy all parties involved.

4. Take a breather once it's over. Once the situation has been resolved, or at least defused, it's important to take a short break (if your job allows it). Step outside for some fresh air, grab a cup of coffee or tea, or simply go into the washroom and splash some cool water on your face. Whatever strategy you choose, it's important that you give yourself some time to cool down and unwind after a tense, potentially upsetting situation.

5. Work on letting things go. After a tense situation, such as dealing with a rude customer, you may feel the temptation to vent about that customer to other coworkers, or even to friends or family when you get home. But experts warn that venting about an upsetting situation can actually become quite damaging over time, if you do it often. Even though it offers a short-term period of relaxation and satisfaction, over time that practice of venting or ranting can inadvertently become the preferred way your brain deals with stress and anger. That can become unhealthy for you, and it could become frustrating for your friends, family, and coworkers.

- Think positive thoughts about yourself. Let yourself feel good about having defused a stressful situation without losing your cool.

- Remove self-doubt by looking at the facts. This may be difficult, but it's important to take yourself out of the equation and recognize once again that the customer wasn't necessarily mad at you, and most likely didn't mean anything rude that was said. That customer was simply upset with the situation, and you happened to get caught in the crossfire.

6. Work to prevent future problems. Ask yourself honestly whether or not anything could have been done differently to prevent the problem. Don't beat yourself up about it, just determine whether you or your coworkers could have done something differently. Then, use the unpleasant confrontation as a learning experience. You successfully acknowledged the problem, addressed it, and resolved it--that's something worth feeling good about. Next time it will be easier, and you'll know how to manage unpleasant customers.

How to Deal with Aggressive Customers

Aggressive customers can be a nightmare. Don't confuse them with assertive customers who simply insist on their rights; this article is about the customers who issue threats, shout, ruin the experience for other customers, and make unreasonable demands. They may even grow physically aggressive by putting their hands on employees or causing damage to property. If you work in the service sector, it's smart to educate yourself on how to deal with aggressive customers.

Part 1

Defusing the Situation

1. Stay calm. The worst thing you can do in this situation is to raise your energy level to theirs, at it might turn a combustible situation into an all-out explosion. However, because you, as an employee, cannot simply walk away from the situation, you must stay engaged with the customer without letting your own temper get out of hand.

- The most obvious thing to avoid is raising your voice.
- Don't be sarcastic with the customer.
- Do your best to maintain a soothing voice and mask any frustration you might feel.

2. Control your own body language. It's easy to read the nonverbal cues of aggression and anger in other people's bodies, but be aware of the messages your own body is sending to the customer. It's not enough to simply keep your voice down — you must soothe the customer's mood with all the communicative devices in your toolbox. Some nonverbal cues to control and avoid include:

- Pacing
- Drumming your fingers or tapping your feet
- Clenching your fists
- Clenching your jaw
- Rolling your eyes
- Furrowing your eyebrows
- Staring the customer down
- Crossing your arms or putting your hands on your hips

3. Don't enter the customer's physical space. Even when everyone's calm, violating someone's personal space can be interpreted as a show of aggression or lack of care for someone's level of

comfort. When people get angry, they need a larger area of personal space, so give aggressive customers wide berth. Otherwise, they may think you're trying to show aggression of your own, or that you're not taking the situation seriously by failing to recognize how agitated they've grown.

- For your own personal safety, try to stand behind a counter, table, or other barrier to reinforce the physical distance between you and the customer.

4. Listen to the customer's grievance. Understand that no matter how unreasonable the customer is being in terms of the scale of their anger, there may very well be a kernel of truth to what they're saying. By letting the customer air their grievance, you're letting them vent off some of their frustration and hopefully stopping the situation from getting worse. Furthermore, you're showing them that you, as an employee, care about the customer's experience, gaining you good will.

- Don't ever interrupt the customer, even if you want to respond to something they've said.

- Even if they're being unreasonable, allow them to talk themselves out.

- Use positive nonverbal communication cues to demonstrate that you're actively listening and engaging with the customer. Examples include maintaining eye contact (but not staring), nodding along, and demonstrating concern on the customer's behalf at the appropriate moments with facial expressions.

5. Ask questions to better understand the problem. In order to calm a customer down, you need to understand why they're upset in the first place. If the customer is so worked up that they're

ranting instead of providing you with useful information that you could use to assess and resolve the situation, wait until there's a gap in the conversation to ask guided questions that will help you understand what's going on. Again, don't cut the customer off — wait for an opportunity for you to speak. Some questions you might ask include:

- "Is this the first time you've had this issue at our business? Can you tell me more about your previous frustrations, so I know specifically how to instruct our staff how to improve customer experience?"

- "Tell me exactly what happened today, from the beginning. What was the exact employee behavior that triggered your bad experience?"

- "Was there a single action that ruined your experience with us, or are you frustrated by the buildup of several small problems? Is there one large thing we need to change, or several small adjustments?"

- "Which employee or employees are you upset with right now? Is there one person in particular, or does our whole staff need to be addressed about their attitudes and performance?"

- If another employee is involved, use your discretion to determine whether or not it would calm the customer down to involve that employee in the conversation.

6. Try to find a solution to the problem. Ask the customer what you could do to make them feel better about the situation. If what they ask is reasonable and within your power, give them what they ask for. However, aggressive customers are sometimes irrational in their demands, or ask you to do something you are not authorized to do.

- Try to strike a compromise. Explain to the customer that you would give them what they want if you were authorized to do so, but that you would be punished yourself if you did that. Instead, offer them whatever you're authorized to give.

- Call a manager. If the customer would like something that you're not authorized to provide, call a manager or supervisor to see if it can be authorized.

Part 2

Ejecting a Customer

1. Lay out the repercussions for their behavior. If you feel like a situation is getting out of control and either threatening your personal safety or the positive experience of your other customers, tell the angry customer that you will ask them to leave if they don't control their frustration. Everyone loses their temper from time to time, so give them a chance to get a handle on it. Remain respectful and calm; don't raise your voice or point your finger at them. Simply tell them what the next steps will be if their behavior doesn't change. Some things you might say include:

- "I understand that you're frustrated, but we both need to be calm to resolve this situation."

- "Your frustration at your bad experience is now making the experience worse for the rest of our customers. We'd like to work with you to fix the situation, but don't you agree that the rest of the people here have a right to a pleasant experience too?"

2. Explain why you're asking them to leave. Customers often take the slogan "the customer is always right" to heart, not realizing that the customer can very often be wrong. Explain to the customer that their abusive behavior is personally threatening, and that they are ruining the experience for all of their other customers, who have just as much right to good service as they do.

- "While you have a right to voice your concerns, you do not have a right to be abusive towards our staff."

- "I am happy to work with you to resolve this situation, but your behavior is making me feel uncomfortable."
- "As an employee, it's my job to protect my colleagues and patrons, so I have to ask you to leave the building."
- "If you don't remove yourself from this situation voluntarily, I'll have to call the police to protect my staff and customers."

3. Escort the customer out of the establishment. To reinforce your verbal ejection of the customer, move toward the exit yourself and ask the customer to follow you. Even if the customer does not initially respond to the ejection, lead the way. Do this even if the customer does not take your lead and move toward the exit at first; when they see that the object of their anger is moving away, they will likely follow you toward the exit.

- The objective is to remove the customer from the premises in order to protect both the safety and the experience of the people in your business.
- Often, when the customer finds themselves removed from the business, they will move on even if they are still upset.
- Allow them to move away from the business on their own before you return to work. If they see you immediately go back inside, they might follow you back in.

4. Don't put your hands on the customer. Unless you feel that the customer has grown physically

threatening to you, other employees, other customers, or themselves, avoid touching the customer. Touching someone who is overly agitated could cause them to react very poorly, and potentially violently.

- However, if the customer becomes physically aggressive either to you, someone else, or to themselves, you are within your rights to try to prevent injury by subduing them.

5. Call security or the police if necessary. If you don't feel safe around the customer or if the situation is disrupting your business and doesn't have an end in sight, call the police or a security service if your business pays for one. Try to limit the customer's impact by getting them outside of your business. Don't try to physically detain the customer, as you don't have any legal right to do so unless they physically attack someone.

- If the customer puts their hands on someone or breaks property, do your best to get them out of your establishment. If they won't leave, move employees and customers away from the aggressive customer to protect them from physical harm.

- Stay calm and respectful, but do not try to engage the customer any further. You've done everything you can to resolve the situation, and you should just disengage and wait for the authorities.

- Keep the phone numbers for security easily accessible for the entire staff instead of keeping them in the back office. When customers get out of hand, employees almost always call the onsite manager to deal with the situation. If the situation truly gets out of hand, there's a good chance the manager is already busy with it, so all employees need to know how to reach out for help.

- Post the phone numbers somewhere out of the way of customer traffic, but regularly visited by employees — behind a cash register, or in an employee break room, for example.

- Make sure the number is clearly legible. If you have bad handwriting, print the number out using a computer.

6. Use discretion when asking a drunk customer to leave. If you work in a restaurant or bar that served enough alcohol to a customer to get them to that state, you may be held responsible for that person's actions once they leave your establishment.

- If the customer seems drunk, offer to call them a cab while they wait outside.
- If they are with a group, ask a sober friend to drive them home.
- If they insist on driving themselves, write down a description of the car including the tag number, and call the police immediately with that information.

How to Handle Customer Complaints Quickly

Customer service is the interaction a person experiences when conducting business with a company or an individual. The experience can be positive or negative. Successful businesses train their staff on how to handle customer complaints quickly.

Part 1

Understanding the Problem

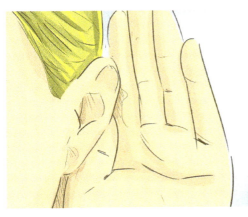

1. Listen to the customer concerns. Generally, concerns over an issue can be handled without it

becoming a complaint. The manner in which the concern is handled will determine the intensity of the problem. Get the customer's name, address, phone number, and any other applicable information like an account number or username.

- The important part here is to respond quickly and professionally. Give the customer a chance to air their grievances as soon as possible. Be proactive in looking for a resolution to the issue.

2. Give the customer an opportunity to explain the problem without interruptions. Constantly interrupting the customer will only add fuel to the problem and may end in a shouting match. It also simply make the customer think that you don't genuinely care about the issue.

- When they're done, repeat their major points of concern back to them to let them know that you've understood.

3. Don't challenge their complaint. Even if what the customer is saying has no basis in reality and you immediately want to completely reject everything they've said, don't tell them they are wrong. This won't help you resolve the problem. Instead, let them know that you understand their complaint without agreeing with them.

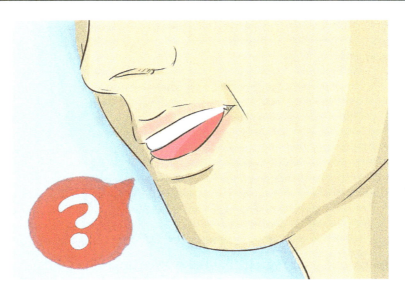

4. Ask questions to clarify the problems and the causes. Next, you'll have to identify exactly where the customer ran into an issue. Many times, customers will assess the entire customer service experience negatively, even if they only had a problem with one part of it. Ask them more questions to determine exactly where something went wrong.

- Many times the problem may not be with the price, merchandise, or service, but with an employee's negative attitude while dealing with the customer.

5. Transfer the customer to someone else if necessary. In some cases, you may be unable to handle the customer's complaints directly. If this is the case, immediately transfer them to someone who can, like a manager or customer service specialist. This should be done as soon as you determine the need to transfer, not after you've already asked the customer a ton of questions.

- If language is a problem, find someone that speaks the customer's language for clear communication to expedite matters.

Part 2

Resolving the Issue

1. Apologize sincerely. Extend your regrets that the service or product did not meet the customer's expectations. Make your apology as sincere as possible. If there business is directly at fault, be the first to acknowledge this. However, if the customer is at fault, allow them to realize this on their own and then gracefully move past it.

- While it may be tempting, don't automatically take an employee's side against the customer or vice versa. You'll have to investigate the problem further to determine who is at fault.

2. Empathize with their problem. Put yourself in the customer's place. Everyone has experienced bad service at some point. Saying that you understand and feel for the customer's problem will help diffuse a situation. Doing so lets the customer know that you're with them and will work with them to solve the problem at hand.

3. Find out how the customer wants the issue resolved. Simply ask the customer what they want,

even if you are unsure if you can provide it. The resolution could be in the form of a replacement, refund, exchange, store credit or discount on price.

4. Reassure them that the problem will be taken care of. Explain to the customer that all feedback by a customer is valued by the company. The customer will be unsure whether or not you will actually solve their problem, so be clear that you intend you reach a mutually beneficial solution.

5. Do your best to remedy the complaint. If possible, go through with what the customer has asked for. If this is not possible, you should offer them other sufficient solutions that may remedy the issue. Focus on what you can offer them instead of on what you can't. Decide on a solution and execute that solution as quickly as possible.

- If the customer's request can be met, explain the time it takes to process or what it will entail to make it happen.

- When a date for resolution is given to the customer, make sure the date is kept, or the delay is explained by a follow-up call or email.

6. Thank the customer. Express your genuine appreciation to the customer for sharing their complaint. Explain that customer complaints serve as constructive criticism and can allow the company to better serve other customers. Be sure that you include that you hope to serve them again soon.

7. Follow up with them. Call or email the customer to make sure that they felt as though their issue was completely resolved. Give them a contact number to call if they feel as though their problem was not resolved. You can also follow up with a customer service survey that you can use to assess your business's ability to resolve customer complaints. This should be done 24 to 48 hours after the complaint was resolved.

8. Record the customer interaction. Write down information regarding the interaction with the customer and how the situation was handled, if applicable. You should also note whether or not the interaction resulted in a resolution of the complaint and what that resolution entailed. Then, compile similar complaints by grouping them under similar categories based on cause or the product/service complained about.

- From here, you can analyze where your receive the most complaints and look to the resolutions to correct the problem for customers before it arises.

- You can also use the complaint-resolution data to analyze how successful your customer service is or how much more or less successful it has become over time.

Part 3
Following General Guidelines

1. **Know what not to say to the customer.** Some phrases will just anger customers more and are not particularly useful in resolving complaints. Here are some examples:

    - **According to our policy...** When mistakes happen, customers don't want to hear about your policies and regulations. Policies keep companies running smoothly and shouldn't be used for hiding mistakes. At the same time, know how to get your policy across in layman's terms.

    - **Let me transfer you to the manager.** Don't throw the hot potato to your manager if you don't need to. Not only you're adding fuel to the fire by forcing the customer to repeat their problem, but you're also showing a lack of competence in your support. If this needs to be done, do it before the customer has fully explained their problem.

        o Be sure to also explain why you are transferring them. For example, you may need a specialist to take care of their problem.

2. **Don't take it personally.** It may be tempting to take all customer complaints personally. If you're

a small business owner they will get to you and make you question many aspects of your operation. However, you have to know that customer complaints are a simple truth of business and that they occur regularly even for the most well-run and successful businesses. Keep in mind that every complaint can be an opportunity for improvement.

How to Handle Customer Complaints about Food

If the food you serve is cold, late, or just wrong, customers will let you know. Responding appropriately in these situations is important if you want to recover your public image and keep that customer's business. Listening, apologizing, and correcting the problem will ensure your dining establishment stays respected and maintains its position as a top contender for consumer dollars.

Part 1

Identifying the Problem

1. Listen to the guest. Let the customer say everything they need to say. If they are interrupted, they may feel the need to start over. Nod to show you're actively engaged in what they have to say and that you empathize with their predicament. Be attentive but relaxed. Look the customer in the eye as they speak.

- Keep an open mind when listening to the customer. In other words, don't listen for what you think the problem is or might be. Rather, hear the customer out and understand their actual problem or issues.

- Don't contradict or argue with what the customer says. Even if they are wrong, informing them of their error will only exacerbate their frustration.

- Do not minimize the customer's complaint. Do not, for instance, say "Sometimes food is a little cold when it comes out. It's no big deal." This will not make the customer happy.

2. Try to picture the problem as the customer explains it. For instance, a customer may say, "I was eating my soup and there were several little peas in it which were quite hard." In your mind's eye, envision the soup in question. Imagine the peas. Are they large or small? Round and smooth, or somewhat dimpled? Are they bright green, or more of a pine color? Finally, the texture. Imagine you have several between your hand which are soft and pliant. Several others are hard and undesirable in soup. You will better understand the customer's problem armed with this mental vision.

3. Clarify what the customer says. There are two ways to clarify a customer complaint in order to better understand and handle it. The first way is to ask questions about the complaint. The second way is to repeat the customer's complaint back to them in different language.

- For instance, if you've just arrived for your shift and a customer is complaining about the soup, you might not know what soup the customer is referring to. Ask questions as needed. You might inquire, "Did you have the pea soup or the vegetable noodle?" Don't assume which menu item the customer is talking about; always follow up by asking for specifics as they explain their issue.

- Once the customer's complaint has been explained, repeat it back to them in different language. For instance, the customer might complain that the food was cold. You could, after hearing the explanation, summarize their problem by saying, "So your food did not arrive at the temperature you wanted it to be at? Is that right?" If they agree, you've listened well and can move on to fixing the problem.

4. Stay calm and show you're concerned. Do not smile or laugh while listening to the customer's complaint. Adopt a solicitous, concerned facial expression. Furrow your brow slightly in the center and turn down the corners of your mouth. This will make the customer feel as if you are truly concerned about what they have to say.

- Even if the customer is using profanity or yelling rudely, do not respond in kind. Exercise patience and compassion. Listen patiently to the entirety of the customer's complaint.

- If they are being particularly boisterous, direct the customer to follow you into a more private quarter of the dining establishment. There you can continue to listen to their tirade without drawing negative attention to the situation or disrupting the other diners.

Part 2

Acting on the Complaint

1. Apologize to the customer. An apology is an acknowledgment that you made a mistake. Tell the customer, "I am so sorry for the error." This will make the customer more inclined to forgive you and/or your restaurant. Be specific in your apology. If the soup was too cold, say "I am sorry the soup was too cold." If the order was wrong, say, "I am sorry I brought you the wrong order."

- Always act sincere when apologizing, even if there is no real reason for you to apologize. It will make the customer feel better.

- Many customers appreciate an explanation, but do not appreciate excuses. For instance, you could say "I'm sorry, the line cook was confused about your order. I'll fix it immediately." But do not say, "The line cook mixed it up, not me. Just hang on while he fixes it." Maintain a sense of personal responsibility even if the problem is not your fault, and avoid excusing yourself or anyone else.

- If you are very sorry, emphasize how sorry you feel by saying "I am very sorry this happened."

- Apologies work online too. If your establishment is active on review sites you can write apologies in response to bad experiences. Write something like, "We are sorry you had a bad experience in our dining establishment. I can understand why you were frustrated. We will investigate this matter in depth to ensure it does not happen again. Thank you for bringing it to our attention."

2. Act quickly when handling a complaint. When a customer has a complaint, no matter how serious, correcting it should take priority over anything else. If a customer is waiting to order and another customer has a complaint, the customer with the complaint should be helped first. Only after their complaint has been heard and an apology issued should the other customer's order be taken.

- If the customer's complaint involved re-making a dish, ensure that this remake goes to the front of the order list in the kitchen. Let kitchen staff know that they need to make the order a priority.

- If it is not possible to resolve the customer's complaint in a way which satisfies them quickly or within the time they have completed their meal, get their contact info so that they can be contacted later with a solution. For instance, if the customer orders takeout and doesn't have his order ready when he comes to pick it up, and doesn't have time to wait for it to be made, tell him to write down his name and number and he will be eligible for a free order of equal value later at a time of his choosing.

3. Solve the problem. Solutions take a variety of forms, each dependent on the specific situation. Thinking about the customer's mood, the customer's problem, and the options available to you to solve it will dictate your course of action.

- Ask the customer what they'd like to have happen to rectify the situation. Consult with your manager or coworkers in order to determine how to move forward. If the customer's request can be honored, do so. Otherwise, use the information you received from your co-workers or manager in order to propose an alternative to the customer.

- Think about how irate the customer is. If they're extremely irritated and angry, you should go above and beyond to ensure they are placated. Consider offering them a large discount, 50-100% off their meal.

- If the customers is mildly or only slightly put out by the issue about which they are complaining, offer them a free drink or a free side.

- If the complaint isn't terribly serious but intended more as an informational aside, such as "The table is a bit sticky," you might just need to clean the table up a bit.

- Always follow your restaurant's protocol when deciding how to handle customer complaints. Get your manager's approval before extending an exceptionally generous offer like a free meal.

- Sometimes food just needs to be reheated, sometimes it needs to be completely remade, and sometimes the customer will accept another solution entirely. Regardless, remove the undesired item with the customer's permission.

4. Share information about the customer's complaint with your teammates. For instance, if a

customer says the soup is too salty, you should inform the cook who made the soup. Tell him or her, "One of my customers found the soup a bit too salty. Would you try it to see if it needs to be adjusted?" While it's important for you to apologize and offer something else to the customer who complained, if there is a real problem with the soup, someone else will complain about it too, down the line, and then you'll have to go through the whole apology and replacement process again.

- Speaking with your coworkers is also important so you can understand what kinds of solutions are possible. For example, if the customer wants a replacement side of mashed potatoes, you'll need to check with the kitchen before assuring the customer that you can replace them. It is possible that the kitchen has sold out of them for the night.

5. Thank the guest for bringing the issue to your attention. Many customers might be too considerate or too proud to complain about their experience. The customers who do speak up are giving you an opportunity to improve on the dining experience, whether in the avenue of food quality, service, or dining atmosphere. Thank these customers by saying, "Thank you so much for bringing this matter to my attention."

How to develop a Relationship with a Customer

Creating and nurturing a strong relationship with a customer is key to the ongoing success of a business. Dissatisfied customers, on the other hand, are often put off by what they perceive as a purely "business" relationship to a company. A strong customer relationship not only means that the client is likely to keep doing business with a provider over the long-term, it also means that the chances of that customer recommending the company and its products to others are greatly enhanced. Read on for strategies that will help you to build a solid relationship with your customers.

Part 1

Building a Relationship with a Customer

1. Get to know your customers in person. Getting to know your customers in person is ideal, as many customers frequent businesses run by people they know and like.

   - When you speak with customers in person, ask about their interests and concerns, as well as what is working and not working for them with respect to your own business. Remembering a customer's name, family members and other personal details can go a long way.

   - Taking notes will help you to remember specific details about a customer's feedback, allowing you to learn more about each customer's particular experience.

   - Special events are a good way to meet face-to-face and get to know customers on a personal basis. They also provide a space for customers to ask questions and make suggestions; you will also learn a great deal about customers' needs and desires.

2. Create a database for customer phone numbers, mail and e-mail addresses. The more detailed and complex your customer database, the better you will be able to respond to and meet customer needs.

   - A customer database will contain phone numbers, mail and e-mail addresses, as well as more complex data regarding customer preferences, behaviour, order history, as well as information about how your business is meeting customer needs.

3. Use surveys, polls, and questionnaires to learn about customer preferences and needs. These tools will provide important information about what customers like about your business and what can be improved.

- A customer is more likely to frequent your business if they feel they are heard; surveys, polls and questionnaires will provide a voice to your customer and increase their engagement with you and your business.

- Employee satisfaction also plays an important role in developing and maintaining relationships with customers. Gauging your employees' level of satisfaction, and encouraging their suggestions for improvements in your business, will provide important feedback and contribute to customer satisfaction.

4. Research your customers. Carefully studying your own company's practices and performance, as well as customer information gathered through market research, will help you to identify your customers, their needs and ways you can improve their relationship to your business.

- Asking specific questions about a customer's needs and level of satisfaction will provide important information that you can act upon to improve your relationship to them, as well as improve customer service more generally.

- Analyzing published market research will help you to build a larger picture of particular segments of customers, and provide information you can use to improve your business relationship to specific demographics.

- Depending on the size of your, business analytics software and other types of computer technology can help gather information that will help you to communicate effectively with customers.

Part 2

Communicating with a Customer

1. Communicate with the customer. Establishing lines of communication with your customers is vital to developing relationships with them, and you should utilize as many communication platforms as possible.

- It is important to stay in your customer's thoughts after an initial meeting. Make sure to establish a line of communication with the customer early on, whether through an e-mail message, newsletter, or other means.

- Don't focus exclusively on your company's products or services, or only contact customers when you are trying to earn their business. Updates on events, product or service advancements, or other news will help to build communication between you and the customer that is not strictly based on business.

- Engaging a customer in your business - finding ways of actively involving them in the development and improvement of your business - is an important component of building a relationship with them. Focus on developing two-way communication with customers.

2. Send out a monthly newsletter. A newsletter is a great way to keep your customers informed of products and services, upcoming events and sales. A newsletter can be sent in more traditional paper form, or sent out through e-mail.

3. Develop a social media presence. Social media is now often crucial to engaging customers, so you should be prepared to interact with customers on a variety of social media platforms (often outside of business hours).

- Set up a Facebook page, Twitter account, or use other social media platforms to keep your customers informed. Invite your customers to visit your business profiles on social media.

4. Hold special events, parties, and contests. These types of events will allow you to meet customers face-to-face, actively involve customers in your business, as well as demonstrate your appreciation for their loyalty.

5. Encourage customer feedback. This includes seeking suggestions on new features or products

that would interest the customer, as well as critiques of current products and features. This will not only build customer loyalty, but provide important information about customer needs and customer satisfaction.

- Let your customers know that honest, constructive feedback is encouraged, and be open to suggestions from your customers as to how you can improve your business.

- Always listen carefully and respond in a manner that lets the client know you understand the suggestions or critiques that have been offered.

Part 3
Maintaining a Relationship with a Customer

1. Be honest with the customer at all times. A reputation of honesty and integrity is crucial to building long-term customer relationships. In fact, customer trust can be as important as the quality of the products you sell or services you offer.

- Always keep your commitments. Attempts to earn trust by making commitments that cannot be kept will only hurt the customer relationship.

- Be open and honest about any problems you encounter. If you cannot meet a deadline, have difficulty locating a particular product, or encounter difficulties providing a specific service, notify the customer immediately.

2. Be transparent in your business dealings. This means focusing on providing a complete answer

in response to customer queries and concerns. Be honest in those communications and set reasonable expectations for getting back to clients if you need to do some research before making a response. Doing so leaves the impression that what the customer thinks matters greatly and that the customer is in fact your priority.

- You can create an online resource for customers to track orders, monitor the progress of a project, or find other important information about the particular product or service they have invested in.

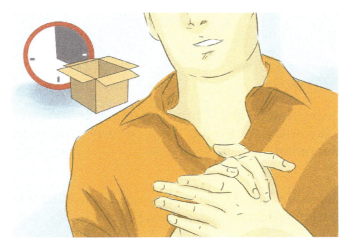

3. Always acknowledge mistakes, problems and delays. Customers will often know when you are telling the truth and when you are not providing all of the relevant information. Long-term customer relationships are built on transparency and trust.

4. Say thank-you to your customers. Showing your appreciation for a customer's business and loyalty is key to maintaining a good relationship with them. Expanding your business requires not only new customers, but also clearly communicating your appreciation to loyal customers.

- Reward programs for frequent customers, particularly for those who invest the most time and money in your business, helps to create loyal customers. Rewards might include loyalty points cards, gift cards, and special sales.

5. Develop a real relationship. Interacting with a customer in person is the best way to establish a relationship and encourage loyalty. A customer's personal experience with you and your business – and their ability to communicate with you in a convenient manner – are important to building a lasting relationship.

- Speak with customers directly. Difficulty reaching a real human being, and the long waits associated with customer service phone lines, can negatively impact a customer's feelings about your business.

- Avoid outsourcing your business social media presence or customer service. Customers appreciate authentic, personal service.

Service and Housekeeping Operations

3

Housekeeping operations ensure that indoors of a building such as a hotel is neat and tidy. Various service and housekeeping operations include making a bed, maintaining glassware, linens, pots and plants, etc. Service and housekeeping operations is best understood in confluence with the major topics listed in the following chapter.

How to Design a Hotel Room

Much like the guestroom in a friend's home, a hotel room needs to function as a home away from home for weary travelers. Before designing a hotel room, do some market research and set your budget. Don't forget to include a modern bathroom, a small fridge, and other familiar amenities into your design plan. Focus on maximizing the feeling of spaciousness and you'll have a well-designed hotel room in no time.

Method 1

Planning the Room

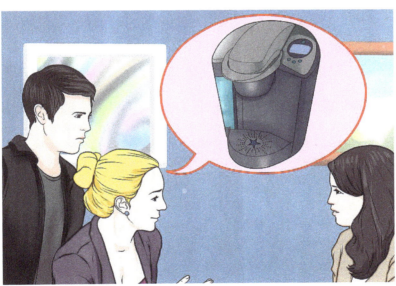

1. Examine your market. Who is the likely clientele for your Hotel? A business traveler is going to have different needs than a family on vacation. For instance, business travelers might expect coffee machines in their room, while families might appreciate hotel rooms that can be connected with a side door. Before you can design a hotel room, you need to evaluate the needs of the guests that you expect to stay in your hotel.

- In addition, watch the competition to pick up on trends and new ideas in the hotel room design world.

2. Determine your budget. How much will you spend per hotel room? The size of the hotel room generally doesn't matter when deciding how to design the room. You can spend a lot or a little on a hotel room of a given size. Once you know your budget, you'll be able to plan the room to your liking.

3. Check your local building and safety codes. Building and safety codes determine things like how many fire alarms, exits, fire extinguishers, windows, and so on a room needs. They are usually issued by a state authority such as the department of public health, and may be amended by local authorities with additional provisions. Stay conscious of required elements when designing your hotel room.

4. Design a mock-up of the hotel room. If you are designing a hotel room for a larger chain, you can probably request funds for a prototype of a new room design. Hire "guests" to try the room out and solicit feedback about their experience to find out what worked and what didn't.

- Have room testers fill out a questionnaire inquiring about every aspect of the room: lighting, comfort, spaciousness, flooring, cover the wall, bathroom, and so on.

- If you are the proprietor of a smaller hotel, you can do similar test runs by designing (or re-designing) only a single hotel room of a given style and renting it out to guests. Administer a questionnaire about their experiences and, if possible, talk to them about their experience in the room to figure out how you can improve the room's design.

Method 2
Creating Ambience

1. Make the room feel spacious. Depending on the size of the room, this might be hard or easier to do. It will be easier to introduce dead space into a larger room than it will be to do so into a smaller room. Fewer things mean more space.

- Add mirrors. Mirrors can create the illusion of space and make the room feel larger than it is. A horizontally-oriented mirror over the bed is a good option.
- Look carefully at the layout of your hotel room to decide what is crucial and what is not.
- Don't introduce lots of chairs, tables, floor lamps, potted plants, or other things that take up space.
- Keep counters and dresser tops clean of excess objects like placards or small statues.

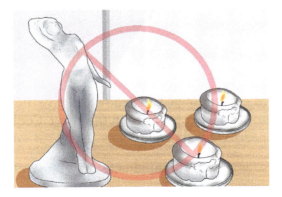

2. Minimize maintenance. Remove things that are hard to clean or could be easily broken. For instance, do not include breakable glass statues or candles that could spill wax on the carpet. Use furniture with rounded corners -- a rounded corner is more difficult to dent than a sharp corner. Remove objects that attract visible dust like study lamps and instead use wall-mounted lighting.

3. Encourage diagonal views. Diagonal views of a room help make the space seem larger. Instead of placing the door in the center of one wall of the room, for instance, place it in the corner of a wall.

- Try to expand the visible angle of the room from the doorway. For instance, if the bathroom is right next to the entrance to the room, cut the corner that is closest to the center of the room from the bathroom's layout (turning it into a five-sided bathroom).

- This is important because people often ask to see a room before they choose to rent one. First impressions are important, and giving the room a spacious feel can encourage potential customers to stay.

4. Choose vibrant colors. Bright lime, orange, and yellow will give the room a fresh, vibrant energy. Warm colors will inspire enthusiasm and optimism in the guest. Cooler -- but still vibrant -- colors like blue and green can also energize guests and impart a sense of safety and comfort.

- Use one dominant color and white highlights to maintain a clean, minimalistic design.

- Despite the temptation to simplify the color selection process, do not paint all your rooms the same color. This way, if a potential guest doesn't like the color of his or her room, you can offer another.

- Do not leave any concrete or brick exposed in the hotel room.

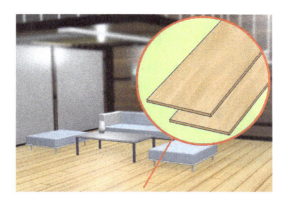

5. Use vinyl floors. Vinyl floors feel that resemble hardwood appear more residential to guests, and are easier to clean. Plus, many people believe that carpets are not clean. Choose a light-colored wood to prevent your room from feeling small and cramped.

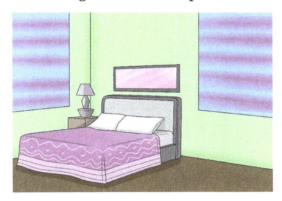

6. Put soundproofing materials in the walls and beneath the floor. Without carpets, the modern hotel room will be even more susceptible to sound leaking out than normal. While total soundproofing is almost impossible, using soundproofing materials can reduce the amount of unintentional eavesdropping guests will have to do during their stay.

Method 3
Providing the Basics

1. Hang a flat screen TV across from the bed. Hanging a TV on the wall saves floor space and makes

the room look more spacious. If you want to get fancy, you could hang the TV in a wooden frame backed with soundproofing material. The size of the TV you want depends on your budget.

- Ensure your TVs are HDMI compliant so guests can connect their devices to watch their favorite shows.

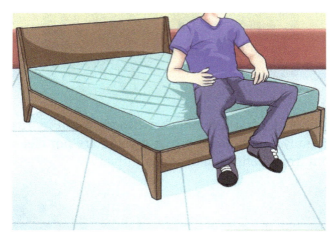

2. Provide a comfortable bed. One of the best ways to provide a comfy bed for hotel guests is to invest in a featherbed. These are both economical and comfortable. Use sheets with a 300 to 400 thread count, and seal them tightly beneath the mattress. Add a couple of down pillows and a duvet.

3. Maximize the storage space. There should be one clothing storage drawer for each possible occupant. If you design a hotel room that sleeps four, there needs to be a minimum of four clothing storage drawers.

- Install a low dresser unit directly across from the bed and below the TV. Horizontally-oriented dressers will streamline the room.

- Do not install a wall-mounted dresser or armoire. These are more difficult to replace and modify than smaller, more mobile dresser units.

- Consider using under-bed dressers if space is limited.

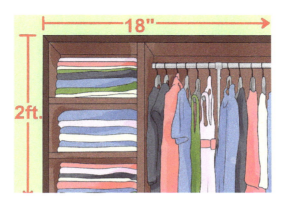

4. Include a small closet. Most people do not use their closet, or use it only for a dress or suit. Keep the closet size to a minimum. A closet 18 inches wide and two feet deep is an acceptable size. The space you save on the small closet will make the room feel more spacious.

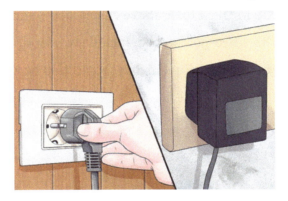

5. Provide enough power outlets. Power outlets are a must for the modern hotel guest. Even a single guest might need three or four to accommodate their laptop, phone, tablet, and/or MP3 player. If you assume some rooms might have whole families together, you can multiply that by three or four. A hotel room should have at least three outlets, plus another in the bathroom.

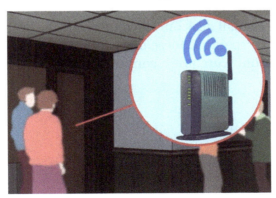

6. Include fast wi-fi for each room. Today, wi-fi is an expectation no matter where you are. Hotels are no exception. Choose a convenient system that doesn't make guests enter their room number every time they log on in order to keep guests connected for the duration of their stay.

- You should also include wi-fi in the lobby or recreational rooms of the hotel.

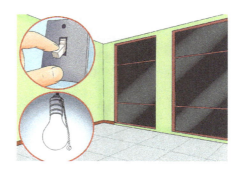

7. Provide ample natural and artificial light. Place a large window at the front of each Hotel room. Use simple, functional light switches and warm white light bulbs.

- Consider hiring a lighting designer. They are usually not expensive and are often provided free along with installation from many lighting companies.
- Provide lighting near doors, next to or above chairs, beds, and desks.
- If designing a room with a two-person bed, include two lamps (one for each side).
- Avoid harsh fluorescent lights. Colored lights should also be avoided.
- Use energy efficient light bulbs.

8. Include a small desk. People use desks less than they used to, but many travelers still have business to attend to and require a small desk on which to work. The desk also functions as a table for guests who wish to dine in their rooms. Choose one with rounded corners and a color scheme that compliments the rest of the room. Purchase a comfortable chair to match it.

9. Include a mini-fridge. Most hotel and hotel guests appreciate having a fridge in their room. When travelers go out to eat, they often want to save leftovers for breakfast. Place the fridge to one side of the dresser.

- You could choose to include a complimentary bottle of water if you have the budget for it.

Method 4
Designing the Bathroom

1. Deconstruct the bathroom. Place the shower and toilet in the bathroom. Place the sink and mirror in small zone just outside the bathroom, facing toward the beds and the rest of the room. This way, when two people stay in the room, one can do their makeup or shave while the other takes a shower.

2. Use a diagonal entrance. Locating the bathroom door on a diagonal angle will not only widen the visible space of the main room, it will make the bathroom itself seem larger. A bathroom of four to six square meters should be sufficient.

- Don't make the bathroom door face the toilet. Instead, make it face the shower and/or sink.

3. Limit the number of accessories. Too many accessories -- soaps, lotions, hair dryers, and so on

-- can make the bathroom seem cluttered. If you want to include a lot of accessories, tuck them away in retractable drawers or under the sink where they won't add unnecessary clutter to the bathroom.

- One large bathroom rug is enough.
- Hang towels on a rack.

How to make a Hotel Bed

Part 1

Preparing the Bed

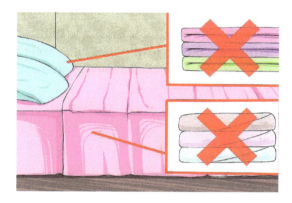

1. Remove everything from the bed. To begin achieving that perfect hotel-like bed experience, you need to start from scratch.

- Starting with a blank slate will get you in the mindset of creating that perfect, clean, and comfortable bedding experience.
- It will also help you make your bed correctly, going step by step.

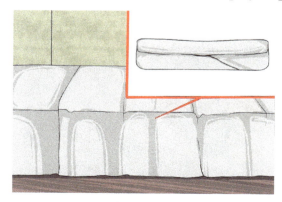

2. Grab clean bedding. To get the most out of making the bed, and feel your best when it's complete, use nice clean bedding.

- Nothing is quite as relaxing as slipping under crisp clean sheets when it's time for bed. Clean bedding will not only make the bed look crisp and help the guest feel refreshed, but it will be easier to lay down and get right.

3. Gather all the blankets, pillows, and sheets. Gather up all the bedding and place it together next to the bed.

- Try making stacks of similar items keeping everything organized and increasing your workflow.
- For example, stack the bedding in order of when you need it. Put all the sheets together first. Keep all the pillow cases together and close to the pillows.
- You may also want to iron the bedding like the sheets and pillow cases to make the hotel bed look attractive. Ironing will get rid of any wrinkles and creases, allowing the guests to experience a smooth crisp flat surface to rest on.
- Thread count will somewhat factor in how comfortable the sheets are. But the type of material and thread length of thread are the real factors. Sheets with a thread count between 500 and 800 are generally considered to be more of a premium quality.
- When looking for sheets, pure 100 percent Egyptian cotton will be the softest and likely most expensive. 100 percent Pima cotton will also be extremely comfortable, though not quite the same quality as Egyptian cotton.
- Look for bedding that also has a longer thread. Shorter threads can poke out of the stitching and feel scratchy.

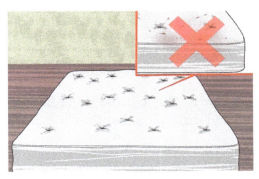

4. Make sure the mattress is free of dirt, dust, and debris. Since you're starting with a blank canvas, make sure that your mattress is clean as well.

- To clean the mattress, use the upholstery attachment on the vacuum. Press down firmly and go over the top and size of your mattress. Remove stains with an upholstery stain remover.

- Vacuuming and lifting stains from the mattress will also rid it of dust mites and odors which could otherwise cause allergies and affect the quality of sleep.

Part 2
Making the Bed

1. Put the fitted sheet on the bed. Start with the clean and crisp fitted sheet. This is the sheet that has the rounded elastic corners.

- Place the sheet around the mattress and pull it taught in each corner. The elastic portion of each corner should be tucked in under the corners of the mattress.

- The seam at each corner of the sheet should be in the middle of the mattress' corners.

2. Lay the first of two flat sheets down. The first flat sheet lays down on top of the fitted sheet. Put the first flat sheet on the bed and make sure that the sheet reaches to the edge of the mattress where the headboard is.

- Lay the sheet down so that it drapes evenly over each side of the bed. Lay the sheet with the finished side facing down, toward the fitted sheet.

- Flatten the sheet and pull it taught on each side so there are no wrinkles.

Service and Housekeeping Operations | 105

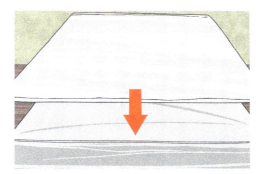

3. Lay a light blanket down on top of the first sheet. Align the blanket to match the sheet.

   - Use a light blanket that is made of cotton or linen.
   - Flatten the blanket out and pull it at the corners to meet the corners of the sheet. Fold the portion of the blanket toward the headboard down to where the shoulders or chest will be when laying in the bed.

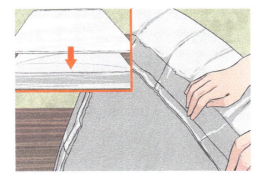

4. Lay down the third sheet. This is the second actual sheet, but the third layer because you've placed a blanket. The third sheet will go above the light blanket. Lay it with the finished side facing down toward the mattress.

   - Align the third sheet to match with the placement of the first sheet. Bring the top of this sheet to align perfectly with the edge of the mattress at the headboard.
   - Flatten the third sheet with your hands and pull it taught at all corners.

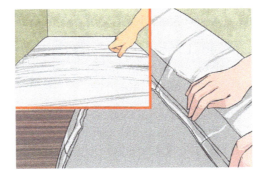

5. Sandwich the top sheet between the blanket and first sheet. Fold down the top edge of the third sheet over the top edge of the blanket.

- Take the portion of the third sheet that extends past the blanket and fold it back so it's now between the blanket and the first sheet.

- Fold and flatten the portion of the sheet under the blanket so it rests perfectly flat.

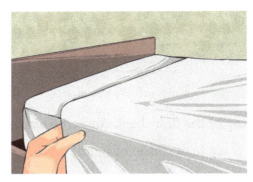

6. Fold the top sheet down toward the foot of the bed. Now take the top of the first sheet which is still flush with the edge of the mattress' edge on the headboard side. Fold the portion of this first sheet that extends past the edge of the blanket and the third sheet back over the top of the blanket and third sheet.

- This portion of the first sheet will now be on top of the other two layers.

- Flatten the edge facing the headboard to givethe bed a smooth, crisp look.

- How far down you fold the sheets will depend on how many pillows you plan to place on the bed. You want the sheets to end where the pillows start.

7. Fold in the corners. Next, you will fold the corners at the foot of the bed. Take all three layers at one corner and pull taught. Flatten the sheets at the foot of the bed.

- The excess fabric that still needs to be tucked under the mattress will form a triangle shape. Bring the leftover fabric down and over toward the foot of the bed. It will create an envelope-like look. Then fold the remaining fabric under the mattress.

- To get a nice envelope look, run your finger down the side of the bed at a forty-five-degree angle. Do this while pulling the sheets taught with your other hand. This creates an imaginary triangle. Fold the triangle portion of sheets at the bottom under your mattress.

- Tuck in the rest of the sheets and smooth to remove wrinkles.

- Do this for both sides of the bed.

8. Place your comforter, or duvet cover, onto the bed. Lay the comforter down with the top edge about 3 inches (7.6 cm) from the headboard.

- Without letting go, throw the comforter on your bed and let it float down on top of your sheets. This motion will allow it to retain fluff.
- Pull the corners taught and equally distributed on both sides of the bed. Then fold the top of the comforter back in a rectangle to leave room for your pillows.

9. Place the pillows in the correct pillow cases and fluff appropriately. Then arrange the pillows to your preference.

- The amount of pillows and styles you use is up to you. The only requirement is that you use the same number for each side of the bed. Place the pillows in a symmetrical arrangement on each side.
- Once the pillows are laid, you may unfold your duvet cover slightly to meet the pillows.

10. Lay a throw blanket down if you so desire. You may add a throw blanket over the duvet cover if you wish to accent the bed any further.

- Depending on the size of the throw, fold it into a rectangle and gently lay it on the duvet cover toward the bottom third of the bed.
- Do not let any of the throw extend over the foot of the bed. It will make your bed look sloppy and uninviting.

Part 3
Adding to the Ambiance

1. Consider the color scheme. If you want the true hotel experience, invest in high thread count sheets and go all white.

    - White is a symbol of luxury and an all white bed will make you feel luxurious and relaxed. White looks clean and inviting and will alter the mind and body to give a quality rest to the guests.
    - Sheets that are 300 thread count or higher will have a large impact on how comfortable they are and how well they rest.

2. Add more pillows. Invest in a few different types of pillows. Hotels offer a range of pillow types to give you the freedom to choose and an ultra-plush experience.

    - Don't overdo it. But create a variety with feather and down, down-alternative, and a boudoir pillow. These options give you variety and allow you to arrange pillows in a way that makes them feel comfortable and swaddled.
    - Five pillows is a good balance.

3. Invest in the mattress and bedding. No amount of preparation and attention to precise detail will counter an uncomfortable mattress.

- To truly get that floating on a cloud hotel bed, invest in a mattress that is right for you. Whether it's a foam, feather, or adjustable mattress. Find one that provides the most comfort.

4. Add a DIY turndown service ritual. You've been diligent and done a lot of hard work to make the bed look perfect and inviting. Make going to bed a ritual that allows you to enjoy your work.

- When it's time for bed, dim the lights. Light a candle, or turn on an aroma diffuser. Then slowly pull back the sheets and enjoy the crisp inviting fabric as they slip into bed.

- To further enhance the nighttime ritual, get rid of any blue light sources. Blue light throws off our body's circadian rhythm and prevents them from sleeping properly. Blue light is often found in screens from our phones, tablets, and computers. Instead of falling asleep to the TV, read a book.

How to Improve Service Quality at your Business

Quality service is a fundamental element of a successful business. But many businesses struggle to improve service and retain their customers. A bad experience can drive a customer away for years. But don't despair! There are several methods to improve quality service at your business, from having clearly defined and measured service goals and motivating your employees, to using customer feedback and updating your service tools to better serve your clients. No matter your approach, improving quality service at your business does not have to be a struggle.

In a Hurry?

The best way to improve service quality at your business is to start an employee training program that focuses on how to be great at customer service. Have experienced employees teach new-hires about your service values. Give your employees goals and recognize when they meet them. For advice from our Business reviewer on how to measure employees' performances and define your service goals, keeping reading.

Part 1

Motivating your Employees

1. Invest in service training, rather than a quality control department. Depending on how large or small your business is, you may already have a quality control department. This department tracks and documents any quality issues and work to address them. But depending on a quality control department can actually set your business up for poor performance, as it may demonstrate to your other employees that quality is not their main concern. Investing in training that trains all workers at all levels, rather than solely in a quality control department, will let your workers know they have a responsibility for providing quality service, no matter their role in the company.

- Look at gaps in service training in your current workforce. Have your employees take a customer service seminar, online, or in person, as part of a performance improvement requirement. Organize training sessions that target specific issues or gaps, such as how to interact with customers at the cash register or how to handle a speech to a client in a meeting.

- For example, if you are trying to improve service at the cash register, set up a training session targeted at improving service at the register. You may discuss how to greet a customer at the register, how to ring them through quickly and promptly, and how to hand them their change or their charge card at the end of the transaction. You may also instruct your employees to do mock transactions, where one employee acts as the worker at the register and the other employee acts as the customer.

- Don't stop training employees after their first few days or weeks on the job. Teach employees that there is always more they can and should be learning about their job, your business, and how to serve customers.

2. Set up a new-employee initiation program. This program will train new workers on quality and service as soon as they start work. It should be a well-rounded program that gives new workers a clear sense of your company's products, services, and core business strategy. It should also reinforce your company's approach to customers and commitment to quality customer service.

- The program should include an overview of your company's approach to service. Give examples of customer service issues you have had in the past and/or are currently dealing with, as well as the solutions you came up with to address these issues. This will help new hires understand your approach to service and how to problem solve these issues.

- Pair up an experienced employee with a new employee. The experienced worker can provide firsthand experience of your company's operations and of how to perform well in a certain position or role. The experienced worker can also give the new worker pointers on providing quality service for customers.

- If possible, conduct part of the new employee orientation yourself. Lead one of the training sessions to show the new employees you are committed to the new hire program. This will also give you a chance to teach the company values in the new hires right away and set the new employees up for success.

3. Teach the 30/30 rule. This simple rule states that the employee should greet each customer within 30 steps or 30 seconds of entering the store. This attention will ensure that your customers feel welcomed and wanted, which will translate to a more positive view of your business.

- Make sure to train your employees to communicate welcome with their body language as well as their words. A "hello" will not mean much if it comes from an employee who does not make eye contact, smile, or stand up straight with open body language.

- If your business is web-based, set up an automatic response system so that your customers know their messages have been received and you are working on solving their issue.

4. Tie your employee's actions to the business's overall performance. This means showing your employees that what they do every day in the workplace has a big effect on customer happiness and the bottom line. Tying individual behavior to a larger system will give your employees a sense of how important it is that they practice good quality service every day.

- One way of doing this is to challenge your employees to commit to providing the best service possible to customers for one month. At the end of the month, show your employees proof of improvement of sales and lower customer complaints.

5. Encourage employees to think of customer service as a "story" about your business. Your employees are the principal way that customers will engage with your business. In most cases, how they behave toward customers creates the overall "culture" of a business or store. Understanding that their interactions with customers are not limited to a single exchange at a cash register, but that they actually inform how a customer *feels* about the entire place, will help motivate employees to provide quality service every time.

- For example, the grocery store Trader Joe's frequently performs at the top of its industry in customer service rankings because employees are trained to provide a friendly, laid-back store atmosphere and offer personal recommendations about products. This approach makes it fun to shop there, which draws customers back even though Trader Joe's stock is usually more limited than other grocery stores.

6. Give your employees service quality goals. These goals should be challenging, but attainable. Research on goal setting has shown that setting specific and challenging goals leads to higher levels of employee performance. Avoid easy or vague goals, such as "just do your best".

- Focus on specific actions and attitudes, like greeting every customer with a smile and a hello, helping them with a fitting room and sizing, and making sure their transaction at the register is fast and pleasant.

- For example, at Harrah's casino in Las Vegas, staff must meet goals that are set up based on the individual's position at the casino, as well as the goals set up by Harrah's group of hotels in the Vegas area. The managers at Harrah's work with the employees to make sure the goals are challenging, but attainable. Harrah's uses a combination of goal setting and future rewards to motivate both the individual employee and the team.

7. Recognize and reward improvements in employee performance. Motivate your employees by acknowledging their accomplishments and their ability to reach or even surpass customer service goals. There are two primary ways to reward employees:

- Financial rewards: One of the easiest ways to implement financial rewards is to increase wages and hand out bonuses to your employees. But if you aren't in a position to hand out more money to your employees all at once, you can improve their finances in other ways. Give them any extra hours they request, offer more affordable health care options, and be flexible around their child or elder care needs.

- Non-financial rewards: Create a recognition program that shows your employees how much you appreciate their hard work and attention to customer service. Focus on a program that recognizes the employee's length of service, positive customer feedback or achievement of a customer service goal. Use rewards like plaques, certificates, company merchandise, gift certificates, or complimentary products. Though these rewards won't necessarily benefit the employee financially, they will give the employee a sense of pride and achievement that is crucial to maintaining her motivation.

8. Let your employees know there is room for growth. Another way to motivate and empower your employees to is to provide opportunities to move up to higher positions in the company or business. Create leadership positions for long standing employees or employees that have demonstrated a high level of performance. Encourage newer employees to aspire to a higher position or role and provide them with opportunities to prove themselves.

- You may decide to conduct yearly performance reviews of your employees to let them know where they stand and how they can improve their performance for the next year. Performance reviews are also an excellent way to reinforce positive behaviors to your employees and show them where their career at the company might be headed.

9. Emphasize problem-solving. It is crucial to emphasize to your employees that they must be helpful as well as friendly. A polite and helpful sales clerk who knows nothing about the merchandise she sells will not satisfy her customers. Similarly, an employee who acknowledges a problem exists without having the ability to address it will not likely impress a customer.

- If the employee cannot provide an immediate solution, train your employees to provide a "plan of action" for how the issue will be addressed as soon as possible. For example, if a customer has called with an issue with a lawnmower she purchased, but your store will be closing in five minutes, you could promise to send a person to her home first thing in the morning to repair it.

10. Teach your employees to overcompensate for any issues or complaints. This is how to attain customer service that goes "above and beyond." Every customer should leave your store or workplace happy. Even if you or a staff member makes a mistake, the customer should still be satisfied. Do not act defensive or accuse the customer of making a mistake. Listen patiently to the customer's complaint and offer your sincere apologies. Then, explain how you are going to solve the service issue for the customer. The most polite employee in the world will not make up for incompetence or an inability to solve a customer's issue.

- For example, a customer comes in with a blouse that fell apart in the washing machine. She has her receipt to prove she bought the blouse from your shop two days ago. The customer demands a refund for the blouse, as it was not cheap, but it did not hold up when washed.

- The employee calls you, the business owner, over to discuss how to best serve this customer. Start by apologizing to the customer for the poor quality of your inventory. Then, explain that though you do not do refunds (as stated on the receipt), you can offer her a gift card to the store in the full amount of the poor quality item, plus an additional discount on her next purchase. This way, the customer knows you have addressed her problem and you will not leave her dissatisfied. You should then assure the customer that you will investigate the manufacturer of the ruined clothing item and pull the remaining stock from your shelves.

- Customers who are unhappy should get incentives to return to your business. This is more likely to create goodwill than solving the problem alone.

11. Listen to feedback from your employees. Your employees can provide valuable insights into possible improvements to your existing approach to quality service. Paying attention to their feedback also shows you care about what they have to say and take their opinion seriously.

- Conduct a quality survey at least once a year among your employees. Send it out by email and set a due date for the survey to be completed. You could also attach incentives or a prize draw to motivate your employees to submit their feedback.

- Maintain open communication with your employees by starting the work day with a pep talk before the doors of the store or shop open. Lay out your expectations for quality service for all customers who walk through the door.

- Demonstrate specific behaviors that show the customer that the employees value quality service, such as how to greet the customer at the door, chat with them as they pay at the register, and ask them if they would like help with a size, or would like to start a fitting room. Use concrete examples to show, rather than tell, your employees how to provide excellent service.

Part 2

Measuring Customer Service Performance

1. Determine how quickly you are able to solve problems. According to one survey, 69% of customers define "good" customer service as having their issue or problem addressed quickly and efficiently. 72% of those interviewed said things like being transferred from person to person or having to explain the situation several times were major frustrations. Make efforts to determine how quickly you are able to address your customers' issues. You can ask about this in a survey. For phone calls or online customer inquiries via email or chat, you can use a timer to determine how long it takes to address the problem.

- Your employees may not always have the knowledge or authorization to solve a customer's problems. However, they should be trained to immediately identify the problem and find someone who can address the issue.

- For example, imagine that you own a beauty store and a customer has called because she wants to purchase a particular brand of nail polish, which you do not carry. Rather than tell the customer "We don't have that," your employee should make an immediate effort to find out how your store can get that polish for the customer and tell her when the problem is solved. This type of behavior is not only friendly, it is helpful and prompt, and it will likely increase customer loyalty to your business.

2. Ask for personalized feedback from customers. Most customers like being asked for feedback. It shows them you care about their experience and are willing to improve or adjust your approach.

- Ask for customer feedback in a personal way, face to face, or via a personalized email. Acknowledge the customer's response with a quick reply. Ask for details about the customer's recent purchases in your store or products from your company that she has used or has issues with. Encourage the customer to explain her experience in your store or workplace and how she thinks you can improve her experience.

3. Create a customer service survey. Customer satisfaction has several key components, such as emotional satisfaction, loyalty, satisfaction with specific attributes of their experience, and intent to return to your business. Creating a survey for customers to take after each service experience will help you determine how effective your service is.

- Track emotional satisfaction by asking questions that determine the "overall quality" or happiness of the customer with her experience.

- Track loyalty by asking questions that determine whether the person would recommend your business to others. People are more likely to trust word of mouth than any other form of advertising.

- Track satisfaction with specific elements of the experience by asking targeted questions, such as "How satisfied were you with the speed of your service today?" or "How would you rate the length of time you had to wait?"

- Track the intention to return by asking questions like "Based on today, would you return?" or "Do you think your choice to visit our store was a good decision?"

- Incentivizing these surveys is a good way to get customers to complete them. Often, unhappy customers will simply not return to a place where they felt dissatisfied. However, if you offer an incentive for them to complete the survey and return to your business, such as a free dessert with the purchase of an entree or a discount on a purchase, they will be more likely to offer feedback and do business with you again.

4. Track any issues or complaints. One way to track the quality of service at your business is to track any customer issues or complaints. Create a database for all customer feedback and use a scale to rank the customer's experience (5 being highly satisfied, 1 being highly unsatisfied). Be sure to also note any detailed comments on service from customers in the database.

- You can also use a net promoter score. A net promoter score keeps tabs on the number of customers who would recommend your business to their friends. A customer who answers 9 or 10 is seen as a promoter, a customer who answers 7 or 8 is seen as passive, and a customer who gives a company a score of 6 or lower is seen as a detractor.

- By subtracting the number of detractors from the number of promoters, your company can come to a net promoter score. The higher your net promoter score is, the better you are doing at retaining your customers and keeping them satisfied.

5. Put processes in place to prevent issues from occurring again. Both you and your employee handled a customer complaint well, and worked hard to resolve it. But just because the customer left happy, this doesn't mean you simply move on. Take this as an opportunity to prevent future quality problems. Ask your employee: "What caused this problem and what can we do to ensure it never happens again?"

- Document the events that lead to the customer complaint or issue, as well as the solution your employee came up with to keep the customer happy. For example, maybe a customer needed a certain dress that afternoon, but there were none in stock in her size at the store. Rather than let the customer leave upset and empty handed, the employee called around to several other locations in the area to try to find a dress in the customer's size and have it put on hold for the customer. The customer then left the store thrilled at receiving great customer service and will be more likely to return to the shop again.
- A possible solution to prevent this customer issue from happening again is to have more dresses in stock in a certain size and to always check the stock list at the beginning of the work day to try to prevent low stock.

6. Talk to customers face-to-face. Avoid the temptation to hide behind your employees. Customers love the ability to reach management easily with their questions, complaints, and concerns. Appear in person at your business at least once a week to show your dedication to your employees and your customers. During your face-to-face interactions with employees, you can also demonstrate how to conduct quality customer service.

- Involve yourself in your business's day to day operations. Not having a physical presence in the workplace can make you seem aloof and out of touch with your business.

Part 3
Defining your Service Goals

1. Consider your business type. Small businesses often have very different customer service expec-

tations than mega big-box stores. Understanding why people choose your store or business will help you assist your customers in getting exactly what they want out of their interaction with you.

- If you are a large company, customers will likely expect a wide selection of goods or services, low prices, and quick "in and out" shopping experiences.

- If you are a small business, personal interaction, knowledge ability, and problem-solving are very important aspects to focus on. You probably cannot offer prices as low as a mega business, but your friendly expertise will make up for it. One study suggests that 70% of customers are willing to pay higher prices if they get excellent, personalized customer service. 81% of customers believe that small businesses provide better customer service overall than big businesses.

2. Create a clear vision statement. Having a clear vision statement for your customer service mission is crucial. You will incorporate this vision statement into employee training and will likely also share it with customers. Your vision statement communicates your business's core values, what you're all about.

- Consider examples from very successful businesses. ACE Hardware, a very successful chain of independently-owned hardware stores, has been repeatedly recognized with awards as being a top customer service provider. Their customer service vision boils down to a very simple statement: "100% helpful." This emphasis on helpfulness, not just friendliness, has helped them compete with big-box stores such as Home Depot and Lowe's.

- Another example is from Amazon, whose customer service vision is: "We see our customers as invited guests to a party, and we are the hosts. It's our job every day to make every important aspect of the customer experience a little bit better." By using a metaphor (invited guests to a party), this vision statement clearly expresses Amazon's goals: to make customers feel welcomed and appreciated, and create a fun and enjoyable experience shopping there.

3. Examine the public "face" of your business. Your employees are one aspect of your business's

public "face," which customers interact with every day. Other representations of your business's mission include your handling of customer service calls and interactions, your location (brick-and-mortar and/or online), and your approachability.

- This article will cover how to ensure your employees' customer service skills in-depth a little later. In general, consider that they represent the face of your company, so make sure that they are trained to be respectful, friendly, and knowledgeable.

- How do customers interact with you? Can they get a "live person" to speak to right away, or do they have to go through automated systems? Studies suggest that customers overwhelmingly prefer to speak to a person rather than navigate an Interactive Voice Response (IVR) system. If you have social media presences, how quickly do you respond to questions or comments on those accounts?

- What does your business location look like? Is it laid out well, easy to access, and clearly organized? This applies to brick-and-mortar locations and your online presences.

- Do your employees and your company structure give the impression that customers are free and welcome to approach you with issues? For example, is your contact information clearly located on your website, and do customers in your physical location know who to ask or where to go with questions?

4. Make sure your employees know what "quality service" means to your business. New hires and experienced workers should all know what "quality service" means to you and your business. This definition may be made up of larger ideas, like "consistency, communication, and connection", or more specific ideas that involve specific actions or attitudes.

- For example, if you own a retail business that sells clothing, your definition of "quality service" may include specifics like "always greet the customer when she walks into the store" or "offer to start a fitting room for a customer if she is holding one or more items in her hand."

- The definition of "good" customer service is highly dependent on your industry and your customer base. For example, a friendly, talkative salesperson might be desired in a retail setting, but customers might not want their massage therapist to be chatty. Similarly, if your customers are older, they are more likely to appreciate in-person service, whereas younger customers may be more appreciative of easy answers over social media.

Part 4

Updating your Quality Service Tools

1. Implement customer friendly technology. Most people do not use cash to pay for goods and services. Your business should respond to the needs and habits of your customers. Invest in a debit and credit card machine to make it easier for your customers to pay you quickly and easily.

- If you don't already have a Point Of Sale (POS) system, consider investing in one. A POS system is computer software that can track purchases made by your customers and what types of products or services they are buying. A POS system allows you to track what your customers prefer, what they like to buy, and how often they buy.

- A POS system will not only increase sales and help you to better market your products or services, it also makes your customer feel well taken care of. POS systems help you manage your inventory, provide special offers or promotions, and give your customer the right pricing. You won't have to worry about accidentally selling customers out-of-stock merchandise or wrongly priced items.

2. Hire a web designer to create a professional website. Your website is often the first impression your customer will see for your business. Invest in a well designed website that showcases your products and services in an appealing way.

- Make sure your website has mobile usage, as many customers will be looking at your website on their phones.

- If you cannot afford to hire a web designer, you can create your own site using Wordpress. Make sure your website features the name of your business, your business' location, your company's contact information and your business hours.

3. Don't neglect your social media. The internet can act as a very efficient service tool for your business, especially if you use social media to your advantage. In today's competitive environment, every business should have a strong social media presence to connect with customers and keep customers engaged in their business.

- Create a Facebook page and an Instagram account for your business. Update your social media accounts regularly and involve your employees in the process of updating and posting on the accounts. Encourage the use of a hashtag for your business, such as #TheShoeStore, to help promote your business.

- Be prepared for customer feedback on social media. Many customers will likely post their customer service experiences on your public pages. This should motivate you to instill a high level of customer service at your business to keep the postings positive.

- Link your website to your social media, such as your Facebook page, Instagram account, or Twitter account. That way, customers will be directed to your other social media accounts, and other ways to connect with your business.

How to set up a Commercial Kitchen

The layout and design of a commercial kitchen will have a significant influence on the functionality and the potential success of any food service operation. Careful planning and research is required in order to ensure cost efficiency and avoid cost overruns. This article provides a comprehensive list of the equipment needed to design a profitable commercial food service operation.

Method 1

Purchase and Install Refrigeration

1. Purchase and install a walk-in cooling unit. A walk-in cooling unit is a cold storage room designed to maintain the standard refrigeration temperature of 28 to 40 degrees (-2 to 4 °C). Although some small food service operations may not require a walk-in cooler, the majority of commercial operations will. Walk-in coolers can be custom built to fit any location. Speak to several HVAC contractors and refrigeration specialists to get the best bid.

2. Purchase an industrial freezer. Commercial kitchen operations typically require freezer space. Commercial freezer units are usually categorized by the number of doors. Purchase a single, double or triple-door freezer, depending on the size and scope of your food service operation.

3. Purchase a refrigerated line station and supplemental refrigeration units. Adequate refrigeration is a necessity in the commercial kitchen. Food service workers need to keep prepared foods cool prior to preparation and service. A refrigerated line station will be required for the majority of commercial operations.

Method 2
Purchase and Install Storage

1. Buy storage shelves for perishable and nonperishable foods, dry storage and equipment storage.

Method 3
Purchase and Install Cooking Equipment

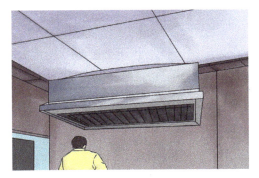

1. Purchase and install an industrial range hood and H-VAC ventilation system. Any commercial operation that prepares food over an open flame, such as a stove top or a broiler, is required to have a range-hood and ventilation system installed. The range hood sits over the top of stove-tops and broilers, and uses fans to pull carcinogenic materials and heat through carbon filters up and out of the building. A range hood can be custom built to fit any location.

2. Purchase or lease a broiler, a gas range and oven, and an industrial salamander. A broiler or an open flame grill is primarily used to cook grilled meats. Commercial broiling units come in many sizes.

- Lease or purchase a combination gas range and oven unit. These units, which are standard equipment in the majority of commercial food service operations, are available in multiple sizes and are typically categorized by the number of burners.

- Consider purchasing or leasing a salamander. A salamander typically sits over the range burners and is primarily used to keep plated foods hot prior to service.

3. Purchase optional equipment depending on the type and the size of the food service operation. Some commercial kitchens will need to purchase or lease additional items, such as a deep fat fryer, a flat grill or a convection oven.

Method 4

Purchase Food Preparation Stations and Small Wares

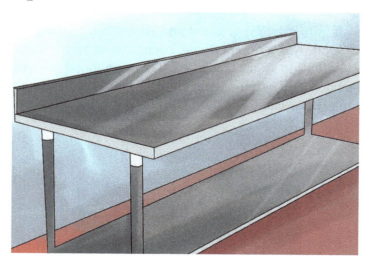

1. Purchase prep tables and approved cutting surfaces for food preparation. Stainless steel prep tables come in several sizes, and are essential in the commercial kitchen. Plastic cutting boards can be cut to fit any size table.

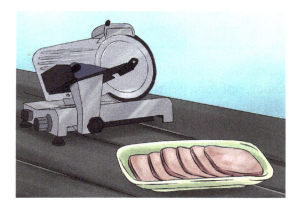

2. Purchase specialty equipment as needed. Specialty equipment may include meat slicers, food processors or industrial-size mixers.

Method 5

Purchase and Install Fire, Safety and Sanitation Equipment

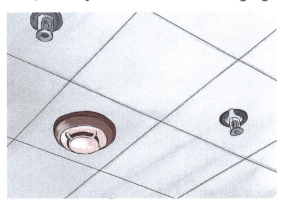

1. Install a sprinkler system and fire extinguishers as required by local fire department regulations. Check with local industrial fire suppression system installers for price quotes.

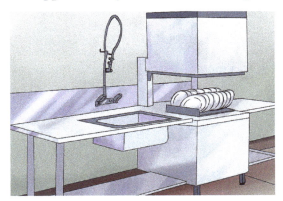

2. Install a triple-sink wash station and commercial dish washing unit. Municipal health department authorities typically require a commercial kitchen to have triple-sink wash station and commercial dish washing unit installed.

How to Clean Drinking Glasses in Hotel Kitchen

Wash glasses regularly with warm water and a minimal amount of dish soap, and allow the glasses to air dry. If you use a dishwasher, opt for a gentle cycle and space out the glasses to avoid damage. Use a vinegar solution to clean cloudy residue or streaks. For dark stains, try a bleach and water soak, or use plain toothpaste to gently scrub the glasses.

Method 1

Giving Drinking Glasses a Basic Clean

1. Clean glasses by hand. Fill the hotel kitchen sink approximately one third to halfway full with warm water and add a few drops of dish washing liquid. Using a clean sponge, gently wash the glasses inside and out. Rinse thoroughly.

- Avoid using more than a few drops of dish soap, as excess soap can lead to streaks and residue.

2. Air dry the glasses. Place clean glasses on a dish mat or clean towel to dry. Position glasses downwards, with the rim on the bottom. Avoid drying the glasses with a cloth, as this can leave residue.

3. Using a dishwasher. Using a dishwasher is a less effective way to get glasses clean and cloud-free than hand washing. If you prefer using a dishwasher anyway, there are ways to improve the results. For more fragile glasses (e.g. wine glasses), choose a delicate cycle. Leave as much space as possible between glasses to prevent clinking or scraping.

- To prevent residue that sometimes remains on glasses after being run through the dishwasher, add one quarter cup of white vinegar to the machine's rinse cup.

Method 2
Getting Rid of Cloudy Residue

1. Make a vinegar solution. If the glasses are cloudy or have white streaks, clean them with vinegar. Fill a medium-sized bowl with white vinegar and warm water. Use two tablespoons of vinegar for every cup of water.

2. Wipe down the glasses. Dip a clean cloth into the vinegar solution. Gently wipe down the glasses with the cloth, both inside and out. Re-moisten the cloth as needed to ensure that the glasses get clean.

3. Rinse the glasses. While the smell of vinegar is strong, it will eventually dissipate after drying. To speed up the process, rinse the glasses in cold water to wash away the vinegar solution. Rinsing the glasses, or washing them as you normally would with dish soap, will ensure that the vinegar smell disappears faster.

4. Soak glasses. If you have numerous glasses to clean, or if the cloudy deposits on your glasses are difficult to remove, soak them in a solution of equal parts white vinegar and warm water. Fill a basin with the vinegar and water, place your glasses in the basin, and let them sit for twenty minutes. After soaking, rinse the glasses with cold water and let them air dry.

Method 3

Removing Dark Stains

1. Make a bleach soak. If the drinking glasses have dark stains (e.g. coffee, lipstick), soak them in a bleach solution. Add one tablespoon of chlorine bleach to a gallon of warm water. Use rubber gloves and protect your clothing from contact with the bleach while cleaning.

2. Soak your glasses. Gently place the drinking glasses in the bleach solution. Allow them to soak for approximately thirty minutes. Remove and rinse the glasses in cold water.

3. Scrub glasses with baking soda. If any stains remove after soaking, sprinkle the glasses with baking soda. Wet a clean sponge and gently scrub the glasses. Rinse them thoroughly and let them air dry.

4. Use toothpaste. As an alternative method of removing dark stains, use basic white toothpaste (i.e. toothpaste that does not contain gels, breath freshening ingredients, or other additives). Use a clean, soft-bristle toothbrush to gently spread the toothpaste all over the inside and outside of the glasses. Rinse thoroughly with warm water and air dry.

Housekeeping

Housekeeping refers to the management of duties and chores involved in the running of a household, such as cleaning, cooking, home maintenance, shopping, laundry and bill pay. These tasks may be performed by any of the household members, or by other persons hired to perform these tasks. The term is also used to refer to the money allocated for such use. By extension, an office or organization, as well as the maintenance of computer storage systems.

A housekeeper is a person employed to manage a household, and the domestic staff. According to the Victorian Era *Mrs Beeton's Book of Household Management*, the housekeeper is second in command in the house and "except in large establishments, where there is a house steward, the housekeeper must consider his/herself as the immediate representative of her mistress".

How to Organize a Laundry Room in Hotel

A laundry room can quickly get out of hand. Spending some time organizing the space can help you wrangle an unruly laundry room. First, come up with an organizational scheme for the laundry. Next, organize laundry supplies in cabinets, on shelves, or in baskets. Finally, create a workspace for folding a sorting laundry.

Method 1
Organizing Laundry

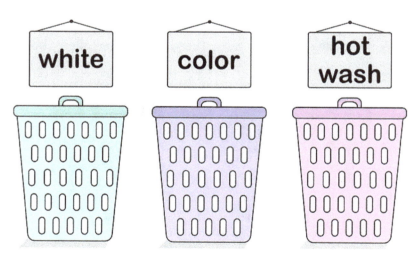

1. Use baskets to sort dirty laundry. Dirty clothing can quickly overtake a hotel laundry room, making it seem drab and unorganized. Try positioning several laundry baskets in the hotel room, with each one dedicated to a particular type of laundry. For example, you could sort laundry into a basket for white clothing, one for colored clothing, and one for household laundry like sheets and towels.

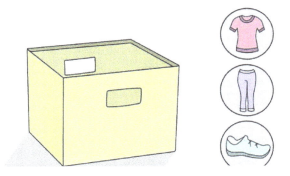

2. Use a bin on the floor to collect grimy laundry. Keep your sweaty running shorts and muddy gardening socks separate from the rest of your clothes. Try placing a canvas bin on the floor and tossing grimy items directly in the bin.

3. Hang a rod to dry wet clothes. Try hanging a shower curtain rod in the laundry room. A rod will provide a space for hanging wet or damp clothing. Try positioning a shower curtain rod above the washing machine, and use it for hanging up clothes that need to air dry.

4. Assign each family member a personal laundry basket. Make sure each member of the family in your hotel has their own laundry basket. Place clean laundry in personal baskets, and ask each family member to retrieve the basket and put away the laundry. Store empty baskets on a shelf. Try baskets with fun, attractive designs to prevent folded or dirty laundry from becoming an eyesore.

Method 2
Organizing Laundry Supplies

1. Make the most of cabinet space. If you have cabinets in the laundry room, utilize them to keep laundry supplies out of sight. Try organizing different types of supplies in separate cabinets. For example, place laundry detergent and fabric softener in one cabinet and use a different cabinet for clothespins and delicates bags.

2. Create more vertical storage space. If you don't have enough cabinet space to house all the laundry supplies, create more vertical space with a shelf or basket. Try hanging a shelf above the washing machine to store laundry detergent and stain remover. You could also hang small baskets inside a laundry closet to store supplies like dryer sheets and clothes pins.

3. Use a shower caddy to organize small supplies. Organize items like stain removers, scrub brush-

es, and laundry pens in a shower caddy. Corralling the items in the caddy will help you stay organized, and make it easier to respond to a fabric first aid incident like wine on a white couch.

Method 3
Creating Workspace

1. Set up a large table. If you have a spacious laundry room, consider placing a table large enough for sorting and folding clothes in the room. The table can also double as a workspace for wrapping gifts, completing school projects, or making art.

2. Try a foldout shelf. If you are crunched for space, consider installing a foldout shelf on the wall or door. You can use the shelf to sort and fold laundry. When you finish sorting and folding the clothes, you can fold the shelf back up against the wall.

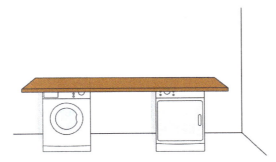

3. Place a butcher-block slab on top of your machines. You can transform the tops of your washing

machine and dryer into a usable workspace with a butcher block. Put the butcher block directly on the machines and use it to sort and fold laundry.

4. Hang an ironing board. If you do a lot of ironing, you can create a collapsible workspace by hanging an ironing board. Try hanging the board on a wall or on the back of a door. When you are done ironing, fold the board back up against the door or wall.

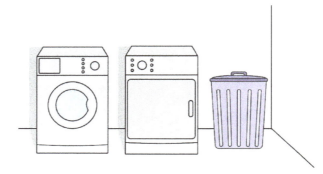

5. Set up a trash can in your workspace. Having a trash can set up in your workspace will help you handle lint, used dryer sheets, and other garbage efficiently. Try setting up a trash can near the laundry machines. For example, you can slide the trash can between the wall and the washing machine or dryer.

How to Dry Clean in Hotel Laundry

Having your clothes professionally dry cleaned can get expensive, especially when you have a lot of items that require special care. Most items that contain "dry clean only" labels can actually be dry cleaned easily with a dry cleaning kit. Learn how to determine which items can be dry cleaned easily, perform the dry cleaning process using a kit, and finish the job to give the clothes a professional dry-cleaned look.

Part 1
Preparing to Dry Clean the Clothes

1. Know which items are safe to dry clean. Start by checking the tag on the clothing item in question. Clothes made from wool, rayon and silk are often marked "dry clean only," and you should have no trouble cleaning them.

- Clothes that are technically machine washable, but that you would prefer to treat gently can be dry clean easily. Try dry cleaning delicate linens and cottons, and clothing with intricate embroidery or other decorations. Dry cleaning instead of washing will make delicate items last longer and look new longer.
- Clothes made from leather, suede and fur should not be dry cleaned. These items require special techniques to clean.

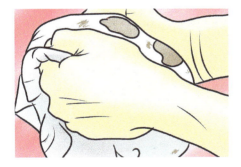

2. Examine how heavily soiled the items in question are. A stain or two is ok, but if the item is covered in mud or another substance, it's probably better to have it professionally cleaned.

3. Use a stain remover to remove stains. Dry cleaning kits come with small bottles or pens filled

with stain remover. Treat oil or water based stains with the stain remover to prepare your clothing for dry cleaning. Instructions that come with the dry cleaning kit indicate to use only the stain remover provider. They also provide details on avoiding the spot spreading and how to avoid a visible ring after treatment.

- Test the stain remover on a discreet spot on the fabric you're cleaning before using it to remove prominent stains. Make sure it doesn't cause damage or discoloration before proceeding.

- Since you're presumably working with delicate fabric, don't scrub the fabric too much, or you could damage it.

- Use the stain remover only on the stain. If you soak the entire garment in stain remover, you could damage its shape and fibers.

- Don't use stain remover on suede, leather, or fur. These materials cannot be dry cleaned anyway, so aren't part of these instructions.

Part 2

Starting the Dry Cleaning Process

1. Place your items of clothing inside the dry cleaning bag. Every kit comes with a bag that fits three or four pieces of clothing. Make sure they are similar colors, to prevent the chance of bleeding dye ruining an article of clothing. When you load the bag, also pay attention to the weight and bulk of the items. The bag should not be more than halfway full. The key is that the items need to have room to rotate inside the bag. If you are cleaning a throw, for example, you may not be able to add three additional items.

- Don't overcrowd the bag. If you're dry cleaning dresses, place only two dresses inside a large bag. You should be able to fit up to four tops inside a large dry cleaning bag. Again, only fill the bag halfway full to allow adequate rotation of the garments inside the bag.

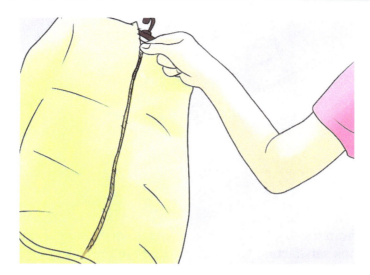

2. Completely unfold the dry cleaning sheet and place it inside the dry cleaning bag. Zip the bag closed.

- The dry cleaning sheet contains a small amount of water, an emulsifier to keep it dispersed, and a perfume to freshen the smell of the clothes.

- As the dryer heats the sheet, it will create steam that infuses your clothes with fragrance and straightens out wrinkles.

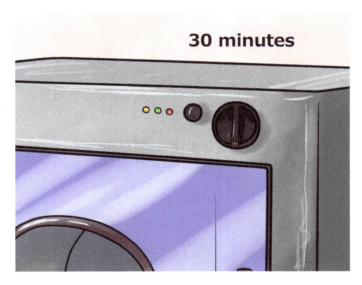

3. Put the dry cleaning bag inside the dryer. Make sure the lint filter is clean. Set the dryer on medium heat for 30 minutes. Use the timed setting, not the automatic setting. If your dryer does not have a medium setting, err on the side of caution and use low heat. If you are using a laundromat dryer, make sure the heat setting is adjustable and use low heat. As soon as the timer goes off, retrieve the clothes from the dryer.

- The longer you allow the clothes to sit in the dryer, the more wrinkled they will be when you remove them from the bag.

4. Remove the clothes from the dry cleaning bag. Hang them on hangers and allow the wrinkles to fall out. If the clothes look satisfactory to you, store them in the closet.

Part 3

Adding a Professional Touch and Storing the Clothes

1. Examine the clothing for stains. You may find that the stain remover didn't quite do the job before you dry-cleaned the clothes. If you still see traces of a stain, use the remover again.

2. Iron the clothing. The articles of clothing won't look stiff and pressed like they do when they come back from professional dry cleaners. Professionals use chemicals to give them that starched look.

- Make sure the iron is set to the appropriate heat level for the article you are ironing.
- Don't spray the item with water, and use steam sparingly.

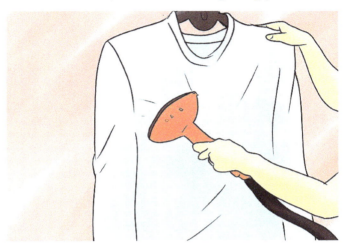

3. Use a clothing steamer. Clothing steamers can be costly, but if you have a lot of delicate items it may be worth investing in one. They use steam rather than the direct heat of an iron to remove wrinkles. The finished look is crease-free and professional.

4. Store the dry-cleaned items separately. Keep them on hangers in a special place in the closet, making sure there is room for air to circulate around them. This way the clothes will stay fresh longer, and you won't have to dry clean them as often.

How to Wash Feather Pillows

Feather pillows can be soft and luxurious, but you need to take good care of them by washing them at least once a year. Washing will help kill any dust mites and bacteria. It will also clean off dust, dirt, sweat, and oils. This article will show you how to properly wash a feather pillow.

Part 1

Washing the Pillows

1. Take the pillow out of the pillowcase. If the pillow is inside a pillow protector (a zippered, padded pillowcase), take it out of that as well.

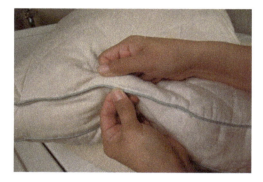

2. Check the pillow for any rips or holes. Be sure to check along the seams. If there are any rips or tears, you will need to sew them back up.

3. Put two pillows into the washing machine. This will help things balanced inside the washer. If you are unable to fit the pillows in the drum, squeeze them first to get the air out. Try not to use a top-loading washer, as the agitator may damage the pillows. If you do not have a front-loading washer, consider visiting a Laundromat; they should have one available that you can use.

- If you must use a top-loading washing machine, put the pillows in vertically instead of horizontally. That way, they won't get tangled in the agitator.

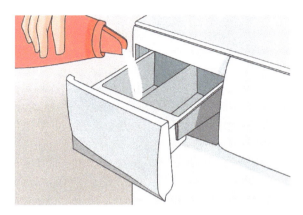

4. Pour a low-sudsing laundry detergent into the detergent compartment. Use less detergent than you normally would. This will prevent any buildup or residue. Also, try to use liquid detergent instead of powder one. Powder detergent is more likely to cause buildup and residue. This can lead to skin irritations and allergies. Pillows are bulky, so they do not rinse out well. The less soap you use, the less you will have to rinse them.

5. Set your washing machine to the delicate cycle. If you can, try to use hot water. This will help kill any dust mites that might be living inside your pillow. Keep in mind, however, that hot water may also damage the feathers. If you are worried about this, use warm or cool water instead.

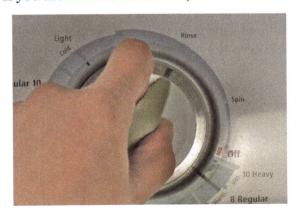

6. Consider using an extra rinse and spin cycles. This will help get any soap residue out. The extra spin cycle will help get rid of any excess moisture.

Part 2
Drying the Pillows

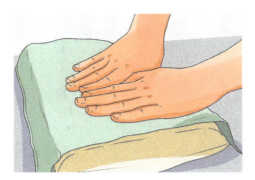

1. Squish the water out of the pillows using a towel. Place the pillow between two towels, and press down on it. The towels will help soak up any extra water. Repeat this step for the other pillow. Do not wring or twist the pillows.

2. Put the feather pillows into the dryer. Use a delicate cycle, with either a low-heat or no-heat setting. Using low-heat will help the pillows dry faster, but it may damage the feathers inside. Using the no-heat or air-only cycle may take longer (and two to three cycles), but it will be the safest for the feathers.

- Be sure to fluff the pillow between cycles. Do this by taking it out of the dryer and beating it. This will also help break up any clumps inside the pillow.

- If you are using a low-heat setting, consider using the air-only setting towards the end of the cycle. This will help keep the pillows from overheating and getting ruined.

3. Add some dryer balls into the dryer to keep the pillows fluffy. If you do not have any dryer balls,

you can use some clean tennis/canvas shoes instead; be sure to put them inside a clean pillowcase first, however. You can also stuff a tennis balls into a clean sock. This will help keep the pillow fluffy as it is drying.

- You can also add a thick towel into the dryer. This will help soak up any water that might be left in the pillow.

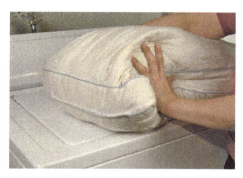

4. Fluff the pillow once you take it out of the dryer. Even with dryer balls, there may still be some clumps inside the pillow. Hold the pillow by two corners and shake it up and down for a few minutes. Repeat this step for the other side.

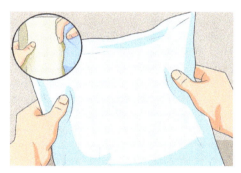

5. Cover the pillows with clean pillowcases once they are dry. Do not use your pillows if they are still damp. Doing so can lead to rot and mildew.

Part 3

Treating Yellowing, Odors, and Mildew

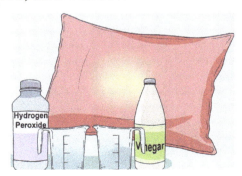

1. Add 1 cup (240 milliliters) of hydrogen peroxide and ½ cup (120 milliliters) of white vinegar to

whiten yellowed pillows. Set the washing machine to a "soak" cycle. Add the hydrogen peroxide and white vinegar directly into the drum. Once the soak cycle has finished, add the detergent.

2. Use ¼ to ½ cup (45 to 90 grams) of baking soda to get rid of smells. Use ¼ cup (45 grams) if you have a front-loading washer, and ½ cup (90 grams) if you have a top-loading one. Add it directly to your detergent.

- Baking soda may also help get rid of stains.

3. Use ½ to 1 cup (120 to 240 milliliters) of white vinegar to get rid of mold and mildew. Add it into the detergent compartment. White vinegar may also help get rid of smells.

4. Try adding a few drops of essential oil into the rise cycle. This will give the pillow a nice, subtle scent. Try something soothing, such as lavender, rosemary, or vanilla.

Service and Housekeeping Operations | 147

5. Think about using pillow protectors. These are padded pillowcases that you put over the pillow. You can then put a fabric pillowcase over these. Pillow protectors will help keep the pillow clean longer, and keep it from getting stained.

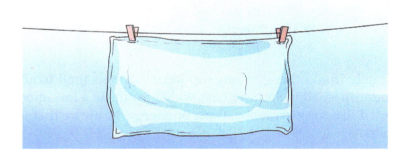

6. Set musty-smelling pillows out in the sun. If your pillow still smells musty, leave it out in the sun for a few hours. The sunlight, heat, and fresh air will help kill any odor-causing bacteria. It may also make your pillow smell fresher.

How to Wash Towels

Washing used towels every week is important to maintain good hygiene and freshness. Towels that have been washed and dried properly will stay mildew-free for longer, saving you money and shopping time. The instructions below can be applied to hand towels or bath towels, with or without a washing machine and dryer.

Part 1

Using a Washing Machine

1. Wash used towels about once a week. Some manufacturers advice columnists recommend washing your towels every three or four days, but if your towels are kept in a ventilated area away from steam, you can keep them fresh with a wash once every week or so.

   - If your towels develop a new smell, or if you live in a damp climate where mildew thrives, you should wash your towels every few days.

2. Wash towels separately from other clothing (optional). Towels tend to absorb colors of other clothing, shed lint, and trap smaller clothes items, which results in a less effective wash. While it's fine to mix loads if you'd like to save money, time, or energy, be aware that a separate towel load will produce best results.

   - You may wish to wash your towels separately if you used them to clean up a particularly filthy mess, so you don't expose your clothing to stains or germs.

3. Sort laundry loads by color. White and light colored laundry items will become discolored if

washed with dark colored items, while the dark items will fade over time. Towels are especially absorbent, so if you want to maintain their appearance you should only wash them in separate light and dark loads. This is especially true of new towels.

- Colored towels should only be washed with the light load if they are faint pastel or pale yellow in color. Otherwise, wash them in the dark load.

4. Wash new towels with special care before using. Wash them before using to remove special softener that manufacturers use to improve appearance, since that substance makes the towel less absorbent. Because new towels are especially likely to lose their color, use half the usual amount of detergent and add 1/2 – 1 cup of white vinegar (120 – 240 mL) onto the towels to minimize later color bleeding.

- If you wish to be especially careful, use this vinegar method the first two or three times you wash a towel.

5. Wash towels with half the usual amount of detergent. Too much soap can damage towels and make them less fluffy. If your load only contains towels, use half the amount of detergent recommended by the manufacturer. If you are washing luxury or extra delicate towels, be sure to use a detergent labeled mild. Detergent typically goes into a tray labeled for this purpose, or is poured directly into some top-load washers.

- Use an ordinary amount of detergent when washing towels in a load with tougher clothing, or if the towels are heavily soiled.

- Instructions should be included on the packaging of your detergent. Many liquid detergents have a cap that can be used as a cup, with a line indicating the recommended quantity to use for a typical load.

6. Learn which temperatures are suitable for which towels. Most white and light-colored towels should be washed in hot water. Most dark towels should be washed in warm water, as hot water can make them bleed. However, if your towels are linen or have a decorative trim or delicate fibers, a cold wash will preserve them best.

- You may still need to wash delicate towels on warm instead of cold if they become heavily soiled. The hotter the water, the cleaner and more sanitized the towels will be.

7. Use fabric softeners sparingly or not at all. Fabric softeners are optional additions to your laundry load that are typically added in a special tray, separate from your detergent. While they make your clothing supple and soft, they will decrease the absorbency of your towels. Only use fabric softener if you are willing to sacrifice your towel's life span for greater fluffiness, and only do so once every three or four washes.

- Consult your washing machine manual if you cannot find the fabric softener tray.

8. Sanitize the towels every third or fourth load with non-chlorine bleach or white vinegar. Add 1/2

cup (120 mL) white vinegar to the detergent once every few loads to keep your towels free of odors and mildew. For a more heavy-duty sanitation, you can use 3/4 cup (180 mL) non-chlorine bleach instead, making sure to use color-safe bleach if your towels are dark in color.

- Bleach should be placed in the tray labeled for this purpose. If your top-load machine does not have a bleach compartment, mix the bleach with 1 quart water and pour into the machine 5 minutes after the load began.
- Vinegar is best added during the final rinse when used for this purpose. Pour it into the fabric softener tray, or simply open a top-load washer near the end of the wash and pour it in directly.

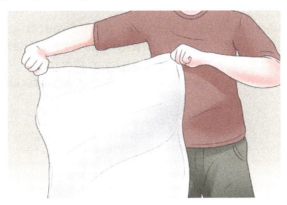

9. Shake your towels slightly between washing and drying. When you remove your towels from the wash, give them a small shake to keep the surface fibers fluffy and absorbent.

Part 2

Drying Towels after Washing or using

1. Hang towels up to dry after each use. Even if you only used a towel lightly, you should hang it up to dry in an area with good air flow, away from steam. Spread it out so there are no bunches and each part of the towel dries evenly. Proper drying after uses reduces the chance of mildew and increases the towel's life span.

- Do not hang one towel over another if either of them are still damp. Each towel needs to be fully exposed to air for proper drying.

2. Dry towels immediately after washing. The longer you let your towels sit around wet, the more chance mildew has to grow on your towels. Dry the towels immediately after you're done washing them to keep them clean. Note that hanging up a towel to dry may take several hours in humid or cold conditions, but as long as they are spread out in an area with good air flow they should be fine.

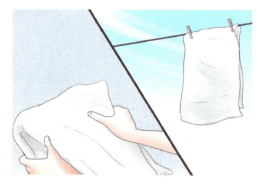

3. If using a dryer, set it to according to towel material. Most towels are made from cotton and should be dried at high heat. Linen towels and towels with a fragile decorative trim should be dried at a cool setting when using a machine.

- Always remove lint from the lint trap before starting your dryer. A build up of lint could cause a fire.

- You do not need to sort towels by color when using a dryer. You may include them in a dryer load with other items, but there's the possibility a towel will trap a piece of clothing and prevent it from drying.

4. Do not put the towels in the dryer longer than necessary. Keeping towels in the dryer after they

are already dry will damage the fibers and weaken your towel. Check on small loads before the cycle is finished, simply by opening the door. If they're already done, cancel the drying cycle and remove the towels.

- If your towels are slightly damp at the end of a drying cycle, it may be more economical to hang them up to dry as described below instead of running your dryer again. If you do start another drying cycle, check on it halfway through to see if the towels are dry.

5. Use dryer sheets sparingly. Dryer sheets are used to soften your clothing. Much like fabric softener, dryer sheets will create a waxy finish on your towels that interferes with their ability to absorb water. If you still want to use dryer sheets for softer, fluffier towels, limit yourself to using them once every three or four loads.

6. Hang clothes in an airy, warm location to dry. If you don't have a dryer, or your towels came out slightly damp from the dryer, you can spread them out over a clothes horse, on a clothesline, or on any clean surface with enough room. If you are used to dryers, air dried towels will initially appear stiffer, but will soften immediately when they touch water.

- Air flow will help dry your towels faster. Pick a breezy location outside or near an open window, but be sure to fasten your towels securely against wind with clothespins.

- Direct sunlight is best for drying towels and reducing germs.

- If no sunlight is available, put your towels in front of (but not on top of) a heater. You could also place them above a heating vent.

7. Only use an iron on linen towels. Do not iron towels made of cotton, or other fluffy towels. Linen hand towels may be ironed if you would like to make them smooth and crisp. After ironing, they may be folded and stored like any other towel.

8. Only store your towels when they are completely dry. There should be no hint of dampness when you touch a dried towel; if there is, you may want to hang them up to dry for another hour or so. When they're ready, fold them several times until they fit comfortably on a shelf without bunching up or getting wrinkled.

- Consider using your towels in rotation to avoid wearing them out more quickly. Alternatively, save your nicest towels for guests and use the rest for everyday purposes.

Part 3
Washing Towels by Hand

1. Learn the benefits and costs of washing by hand. Washing towels by hand saves money, uses

much less energy, and doesn't wear them out nearly as quickly as a washing machine. However, while hand towels are relatively easy to wash in a sink or bucket, large towels will become quite heavy when they absorb water, and will take a large amount of work and time to clean.

- For large towels, the equipment mentioned below is recommended, especially the agitator. However, instructions for washing using only your hands are also included.

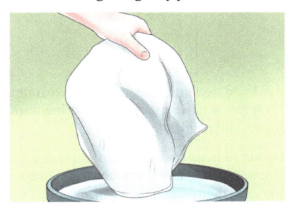

2. Spread out the towels in a clean sink, bathtub, or bucket. Depending on how large your load of towels is, you'll want to use one of these containers. First, make sure the container is clean by scrubbing with plenty of soap and hot water. When you put the towels in, make sure they are all spread out and not knotted or bunched together.

- A kitchen sink or heavily used bathtub may require stronger cleaning methods. Allow bleach or other cleaning products time to do their work, then rinse off thoroughly before using the container as a laundry tub.

3. Fill the container with water and a little detergent. You can use cold or warm water; there is no need to make it scalding hot. Add a small amount of mild detergent. A typical 5 gallon (20 L) bucket requires about a tablespoon (15 mL) of detergent, while a bathtub may require 4 tablespoons (60 mL). Use your judgement and add more detergent if the towels are particularly dirty.

- Use eco-friendly detergent if you will be dumping the water outside.

- Always use mild detergent to protect your hand if you don't plan on wearing gloves. Try to use it whenever washing towels, since they tend to be easily damaged by harsh detergents.

4. Add borax for more effective hand washing. Borax will soften your water and make it easier for the detergent to do its work. It is safe and easy to add to your hand washing session, although you should keep it out of reach of pets and children.

- Try adding one tablespoon of borax per gallon of water (15 mL borax for every 4 L water). You can increase this amount if you are having trouble removing stains, but it's wise to start with a small amount so there is no chance of staining or damaging delicate items.

5. Let the towels soak depending on dirt and size of load. A large or muddy load of towels should be left to soak for 40 – 60 minutes, while a lightly used load that fits in a bucket may be ready in a few minutes. This soaking will save you a lot of effort by removing a portion of the dirt.

6. Press and move the clothes around vigorously. Heavy towels are difficult to agitate by hand, and most easily done using a storebought manual agitator. You can also make your own by purchasing a brand new plunger and cutting holes in the rubber for water to squeeze through. Using your agitator, spend about two minutes (roughly 100 strokes of the agitator) squeezing the towels and pushing them against the walls of the tub.

- If you are washing hand towels, you may be able to imitate this process by hand. Wearing rubber gloves, squeeze the towels together and against the side of the tub. Large cotton towels will be difficult to wash this way, and if you do not have an agitator tool you should expect to spend much longer than the times listed here to get them fully clean.

7. Wring out the towels. If you own a clothes wringer, you can put each towel through it and wring it by turning the handle with as much pressure as you can. Otherwise, twist each towel by hand in both directions, trying to squeeze as much of the water out as possible.

- Use rubber gloves if you want to keep your hands clean.

8. Rinse the towels under fresh cold water and let them soak in it for 5 minutes. You can either move the towels to a new bucket of cold water, or empty the container and fill it again with fresh cold water. Rinse the towels in the running water as you fill the bucket. Let soak five minutes before continuing.

9. Agitate the towels in the same way as before. Again, you'll spend about 2 minutes or 100 strokes

of the agitator pressing the towels against the walls and base of the container and pushing them around. The water should get less dirty this time around, and contain fewer soap bubbles.

10. Repeatedly rinse, wring, soak, and agitate the towels until they are clean. Repeat the process just as you did after the initial agitation. Rinse the towels under running cold water. Wring the towels dry by twisting and squeezing them by hand or in a wringer. Soak them in a fresh bucket of cold water for five minutes. Agitate them for about another two minutes. One more round should be sufficient for most towels, but heavy or heavily soiled ones may take several more sessions.

- When the towels are ready, the water should be free of dirt and soap suds. Leaving soap suds on the towels will make them stiff, starchy, and bad at absorbing water.

11. Wring the towels out as thoroughly as possible. When the towels appear clean and completely free of suds, twist them through the wringer or using your hands. Do this several times to remove as much water as possible.

12. Hang the towels up to dry. If you need them dried quickly, you can of course follow those instructions in the same section for using a dryer

How to Clean a Sofa in Hotel

It is an inevitable fact of life--sofas get dirty. Chip crumbs find their ways into the cracks, drinks get spilled, and pets track mud all over the surface of these sturdy pieces of furniture. Luckily, cleaning a sofa is relatively easy--all you need is a bit of time and some great cleaning supplies.

Method 1

Pre-Cleaning the Sofa

1. Vacuum up large particles. Before getting into the deep-cleaning, you want to remove any surface debris or particles from the surface of the sofa. Use a dust-buster or a hose attachment on a full-sized vacuum cleaner to clear the sofa.

- Use the long, narrow attachment to get into the crevices.
- Vacuum all the surfaces of the cushions.
- Remove the cushions and vacuum the base of the sofa.

2. Use a bristle brush. If there are any spots that have heavy dust or dirt caked in, use a stiff-bristled brush to break up the spots and vacuum up the released dirt. Rub vigorously, but not hard enough to damage the fabric.

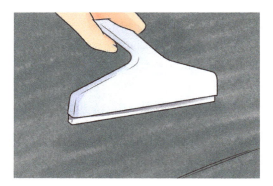

3. Remove lint and fur. Although some companies make products specifically for hotel with pets, the average vacuum cleaner won't be able to remove lint or pet hair. Use a lint roller to remove what the vacuum cleaner can't.

- Work in a systematic grid across the entire surface of the sofa to ensure you don't miss any hair.

4. Wipe down any exposed hard surfaces. Many sofas have exposed wood or other materials, and you want to make sure you give them attention too. Find a cleaning product appropriate for the surface you want to clean. An all-purpose surface cleaner will suffice if you don't have a surface-specific product on hand.

- If the spray zone is broad, spray into a paper towel and simply rub that over the surface to be cleaned. This will prevent getting unwanted chemicals on your fabric.

5. Determine the sofa fabric. Find the tag that tells you what the sofa cover is made out of. These tags usually have instructions for what cleaning products you should use on the fabric.

- "W" means to use a water-based detergent with a steam vacuum.
- "WS" means you can use either a water-based detergent with a steam vacuum or a dry-cleaning detergent.
- "S" means to use only a dry-cleaning detergent.
- "O" means the material is organic, and should be washed using cold water.
- "X" means to either vacuum and bristle-brush alone, or to use a professional service for shampooing.

Method 2

Cleaning a Fabric Sofa with Water-Based Detergent and a Steam Cleaner

1. Pre-condition the fabric. Fabric pre-conditioner might not be found in your average grocery store, so you may have to purchase it online if you can't find it elsewhere. It's used to dissolve and loosen soiled debris and oil for easier removal during shampooing.

  - Spot-test the preconditioner on a spot of the sofa that isn't readily viewable to make sure it doesn't result in discoloration.
  - Spray the pre-conditioner over all the sofa surfaces you plan to shampoo.

2. Make a solution of detergent and water. Mix 3 ounces of your water-based detergent with 3 ounces of water in a bowl or other container.

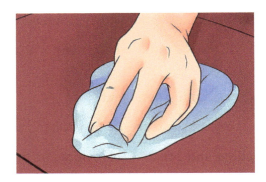

3. Spot-test your detergent solution. Dip a rag into the solution and rub it on a little-seen portion of the sofa. You can use the same spot you tested the preconditioner on.

- Let the solution sit on the fabric for 10 minutes, then check it.
- Press a paper towel to the spot to see if any of the fabric's dye comes off on it.
- If there's no discoloration, move on to the next step.

4. Prepare the steam vacuum. Different models of steam vacuums might look different, so this step will provide very general instructions.

- Locate the tank on your team vacuum, and unscrew the cap that keeps the liquid in.
- Pour the solution of fabric shampoo and water into the tank, then replace the lid.
- Attach the hose if it's not permanently attached.
- Attach the stair/upholstery attachment to the end of the hose.

5. Apply the shampoo to the sofa. Place the nozzle against the sofa's fabric and hold down the trig-

ger or button that releases the solution you poured into the tank. Keeping the button depressed, move across the surface of the sofa in a grid pattern, just as you did with the vacuum cleaner earlier. Make sure you apply the shampoo to the entire sofa.

- Move slowly to ensure even distribution of the shampoo.

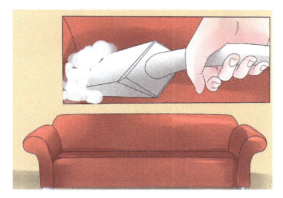

6. Remove the excess detergent. Release the button that applies the shampoo. Move the nozzle across the surface of the sofa once more this way, sucking up excess detergent back into the vacuum.

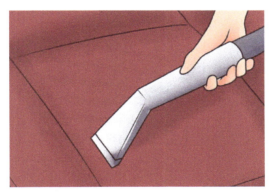

7. Repeat the process as necessary. If there are particular spots that need extra shampooing, spot-treat them with the nozzle. However, don't over-shampoo any area, as it can result in permanent discoloration.

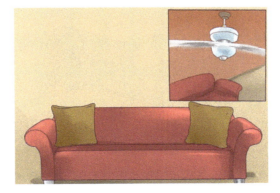

8. Let the sofa air-dry. No amount of vacuuming with the button released will dry the fabric out. Just leave the sofa alone until it air dries completely.

Method 3

Dry Cleaning a Fabric Sofa

1. Purchase a dry cleaning solvent. The name is a little misleading, as dry cleaning products aren't actually "dry." They're liquids — but they don't have any water, like water-based solvents do.

- You may be able to find dry cleaning solvents in the cleaning aisle of the grocery store.

- If not, you can purchase it easily online.

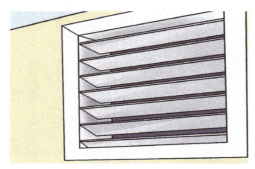

2. Ventilate the room. Dry cleaning solutions have a very strong odor, so open any doors and windows in the area to let the smell escape and let clean air in. Turn on a ceiling fan or set up a floor fan pointing toward the window or do to encourage the fumes to leave the room.

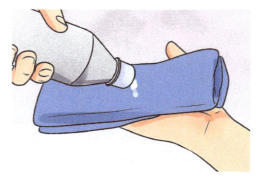

3. Apply the dry-cleaner to a clean rag. Rather than applying the solution directly to the couch, you want to apply it to a rag that you'll blot against the stained portions of the fabric. These solutions tend to be very strong, so remember that a little goes a long way. Follow the guidelines on the packaging for the specific product you purchased.

4. Spot-test the solution. Rub the rag on a small, little-seen area of the couch. Wait 10 minutes and check to see if there has been any discoloration on the sofa fabric. Press a paper towel against the wet area to see if any dye comes off. If not, move on to the next step.

5. Press the rag onto the stained portions of the couch. You don't want to rub the stains — just to press the rag with dry cleaner on it against them. This might take a long time, but don't get impatient and apply too much dry cleaner to the stain. This might harm the fabric.

- Take breaks and allow the solvent to dry from time to time for heavy stains that require a great deal of treatment.

- Reapply dry cleaner to the rag as necessary, but remember to show restraint.

6. Blot up the dry cleaner. If you let the chemicals sit on your stain for too long, they can leave discoloration on your fabric. To remove the dry cleaner from the fabric, moisten a new clean cloth with water. It should be damp, but not soaking wet. Blot it over the stains, re-washing and wringing it out as necessary.

- Once you've finished, let the couch air dry.

Method 4
Cleaning a Leather Sofa

1. Buy a gentle leather cleaner. Though wiping a leather sofa down with a moist rag will work as part of your regular cleaning routine, every once in a while, you should give it a proper cleaning. Harsh chemicals can damage and discolor the leather, so purchase a product specifically designed for leather upholstery.

   - If you cannot find such products at the grocery store, try a larger department store like Target or Walmart. You can also buy these products easily online.

2. Make a cleaning solution with white vinegar. If you don't want to spend money on a cleaner, you can make an effective cleaning product cheaply and easily. Simply mix equal parts water and white vinegar in a bowl.

3. Apply the cleaner to the couch. You don't want to apply the cleaner directly to the surface of the

sofa. Instead, you'll apply it to a rag and use that to apply it to the leather. Wipe the rag over the entire sofa, making sure to work in a grid pattern so you don't miss anything.

- The rag should be damp, but not soaking wet.

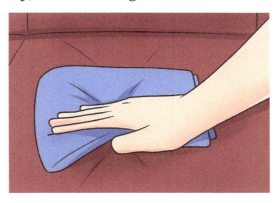

4. Wipe the sofa clean. Use a fresh, dry rag to wipe the leather clean of the cleaning product you just applied to the surface.

5. Condition the couch overnight. Make a solution that's one part white vinegar and two parts linseed or flax oil. Rub that onto the couch in a grid pattern using another fresh, clean rag.

- Let this solution work on the sofa overnight, or for about eight hours.

6. Buff the sofa. After you've let the couch condition overnight, rub the sofa down with another fresh, clean rag. This will make the leather healthy and shiny, like new.

How to Clean Fake Plants

Fake plants are a great way to add color and texture to any hotel or aquarium. These convincing faux arrangements and plants bring the serenity of nature into the hotel without the added hassle of watering and regular maintenance. However, fake plants do require some regular cleaning, or they will fade and deteriorate. Dust your fake plants regularly and apply cleaning products as needed.

Method 1

Cleaning Plastic Plants

1. Gather your cleaning products and tools. In order to thoroughly rid your plastic plants of dirt and dust, you will need to have the following cleaning products and tools on hand:

- Feather duster or vacuum cleaner
- Microfiber cloths
- Cleaning rags
- Hot water
- Window cleaner with Ammonia D

2. Dust the plants. Begin the cleaning process by removing dust, dirt, and debris from the plastic plants. There are several ways to remove dust from the plastic plants:

- Run over the faux foliage with a feather duster.
- Attach a cleaning brush to the vacuum and suck up the dust, dirt, and debris.
- Wipe down the leaves, stems, and pot with a dry microfiber cloth or a wet rag.
- Submerge your plastic plants in hot water or spray them down with a hose.

3. Dry the plastic plant. After dusting your plastic plant, dry the leaves, stems, and pot. You may allow the plant to air dry or wipe it down with a clean, dry cloth. If you submerged your plant or rinsed it with water, this step is especially important.

4. Spray window cleaner with Ammonia D on the plant. To thoroughly clean your plastic plant, you must dust as well as disinfect it. Spray window cleaner with Ammonia D onto your entire plastic plant. Set your plastic plants in the sunlight for 30 minutes. This will help activate the cleaning product and restore your plastic plant's vibrant colors.

Method 2

Cleaning Silk Plants

1. Dust the silk plants. When your silk plants have accumulated small amounts of dust and dirt,

rely on traditional dusting methods to efficiently clean and revive your faux foliage. There are several dusting methods to choose from:

- Run over the leaves, flowers, stems, and pot with a feather duster.
- Attach a cleaning brush to your vacuum and suck up the dirt, dust, and debris.
- Remove dust from the plants with a blow dryer set to low heat.
- Wipe away grime from your silk plants with a dry microfiber cloth.

2. 'Dry Clean' hard to reach dust with salt. Remove moderate dust accumulation from all the nooks and crannies of your silk plants with a simple, yet effective, salt-cleaning method.

- Pour ½ cup salt into a plastic bag—the size of the bag is dependent upon the size of the silk floral arrangement.
- Place the silk floral arrangement inside the plastic bag and seal it shut.
- Shake the bag vigorously for 1 to 2 minutes. The salt will act as scrubbers, removing dust, dirt, and debris from the surface and hard to reach places. Repeat the process as needed.
- Open the bag. Turn the silk arrangement upside down with in the bag and shake it once or twice to remove the salt.
- Remove the arrangement from the bag and return it to its container.
- You may substitute cornmeal or rice for salt.

3. Check for colorfastness before liberally applying any cleaning product or water. When checking for colorfastness, you are trying to determine how resistant the dye in a fabric is to removal. Prior

to applying large amounts of water or a cleaning product to your silk flowers, always test an inconspicuous spot to see how it affects the color.

- Spray, dab, or wipe a minuscule amount of cleaning product onto an inconspicuous part of the silk flowers and observe the spot for changes. If the color was negatively affected, do not proceed to use the product; If the color did not change, the product is safe to use.

4. Remove grime with cleaning products. When your silk foliage is coated in grime, revive your faux bouquets with various cleaning products. Before applying these products, place your arrangement in a sink or outdoors.

- Refresh your faux foliage with a silk flower cleaner, which come in spray and aerosol varieties. Coat the entire arrangement with the silk flower cleaner. Follow the instructions provided on the product.
- Fill a spray bottle with 50/50 water and white vinegar mixture. Spray the entire arrangement with the water-vinegar mixture—don't forget to spritz the backside of leaves and petals. Dab the arrangement dry with a clean cloth. You may substitute rubbing alcohol for white vinegar.
- In a clean 3-gallon bucket, combine 2 gallons of hot water with 1 tablespoon of white flaky soap. Fill a spray bottle with this mixture. Coat the entire arrangement with the water-soap mixture. Dry the arrangement with a clean cloth. If the silk flowers require additional cleaning, you may then apply 1 to 3 coats of non-aerosol silk flower cleaner to your arrangement—allow the silk flowers to dry completely between coats.

5. Rinse your arrangement in cool water. Easily remove a thick coating of dust from your silk arrangements with cool water and dish soap.

- Fill a small basin with cool water—never use hot water, it will melt the glue used to hold the flowers together.

- Squirt a small amount of dish soap into the water and mix.

- Dip one stem at a time into the cool, soapy water flower first. If necessary, rub the foliage lightly to remove grime.

- Remove the stem from the water a blot dry with a clean cloth.

- Repeat on the remaining stems.

- Once clean and dry, rearrange the flowers and return them to their container.

Method 3

Cleaning Fake Aquatic Plants

1. Run your plastic plants under hot water. Over time, algae builds up on the surface of your plastic aquatic plants. Before you can sterilize the fake plants, you must remove the algae. Turn on your faucet and wait for the water to become hot. Place the plastic plants under the running hot water to rinse of the algae.

2. Submerge your plastic plants in a water-bleach mixture. The process of sterilizing your plastic aquatic plants in a water-bleach mixture begins by submerging them in a water-bleach bath for 1 hour.

Service and Housekeeping Operations | 173

- Retrieve a 3 gallon bucket, disposable plastic gloves, protective eyewear, and a bottle of bleach.

- Pour 1 gallon of hot water into the bucket.

- Put on the disposable gloves and protective eyewear.

- Add 1 teaspoon of bleach to the water and stir. If your plants are vividly colored, add an addition ½ teaspoon bleach.

- Submerge the faux foliage into the water-bleach mixture for 1 hour. Stir the mixture every 15 minutes.

3. Cleanse the plants with a chlorine neutralizer. Before returning your plastic plants to an aquarium, soak them in a chlorine neutralizer and rinse with hot water.

- Retrieve a clean 3-gallon bucket.

- Pour 1 gallon of hot water into the fresh bucket. Submerge the plants in the water.

- Add a chlorine neutralizer to the water—carefully follow the instructions on the package.

- After the allotted soaking time, remove the plants from the bucket and rinse your faux plants under hot water.

4. Rinse and scrub your silk plants. You must clean your silk aquatic plants differently than your plastic aquatic plants—exposing your silk plants to bleach will damage the fragile fabric.

- Rinse your silk plants under hot tap water to remove any built-up algae.
- Create a cleaning paste. Measure out ½ cup un-iodized salt and pour it into a small bowl. Gradually add lemon juice until a paste is created.
- Apply the paste to the silk plants with a clean toothbrush. Scrub thoroughly.
- Rinse the silk plant under hot water to remove the paste and any remaining algae.

How to Clean Plastic Plants

While plastic plants don't require nearly as much upkeep as their living counterparts, they occasionally require cleaning, like any other surface in the hotel. This is particularly true if you're receiving guests who have allergies to dust or other grime that can linger on your plants. You can easily get your plastic plants looking their best by dusting them or washing them thoroughly.

Method 1

Dusting the Plants

1. Use a can of compressed air to remove the bulk of the dust. Compressed air (usually used to dust computer parts) is particularly effective for clearing dust off of curved surfaces and recesses. The high pressure blasts off dust relatively easily and the long nozzle allows you to reach around a plant's curves and nooks.

- You may want to take the plant outside before dusting it this way, or the dust might linger in the air.

2. Use a blow dryer to rid your plant of dust. If you don't have access to a can of compressed air,

a blow dryer can serve the same purpose. It might not be as effective, but it can still take care of most of the dust. Make sure to use a low or cool setting, as too much heat could damage the plant.

3. Use a duster, cloth or rag to clean the remaining dust. After clearing the bulk of the dust, inspect the plant for any remaining dust and wipe it away. Pay close attention to the stems and places where the leaves tend to bunch up.

Method 2

Washing the Plants

1. Fill your receptacle with warm water. Ensure the water is not too hot, as hot water may cause your plant's colors to run. If the plant is considerably dirty, you can add a teaspoon of mild liquid detergent.

2. Wrap a garbage bag around the base of the plant. This is especially important if your plant has a deep pot, or simply parts around its base that shouldn't get wet. Wrap the bag around the plant's base, then use adhesive tape to secure it.

3. Swish the plant around to shake off grime. This should be enough to dislodge everything but the most tenacious dirt. Make sure to submerge as much of the plant as possible to clean it evenly.

4. Rub stubborn spots and stains with a cloth. Keeping the plant submerged, dampen a cloth to rub tougher buildups of dirt and grime. Should these spots prove particularly difficult, you can add a mild detergent to your cloth before rubbing. Clean carefully, especially with more fragile plants.

5. Rinse and dry. It's especially important to rinse your plant if you used detergent. A shower head or kitchen spray nozzle works particularly well for this step. Dry your plant by first wiping off excess water with a clean cloth, then setting the plant out to air dry.

How to Clean Pots and Pans

The longer that you let food and gunk sit on pots and pans, the harder it is to remove. You should avoid putting most types of pots and pans in the dishwasher because machine washing can scratch them and remove their protective coating. Luckily, there are easy methods that you can use to clean copper, aluminum, or cast iron kitchenware with soap and water or commonly found ingredients. With the right knowledge you'll have spotless kitchenware in no time.

Method 1

Washing by Hand

1. Fill the pot or pan ⅓ of the way with hot water. Hot water is effective at removing stuck on food and stains. You shouldn't put non-stick, cast iron, or aluminum pots and pans in a dish washer.

- Putting your pots and pans in the dishwasher may scratch and damage them.

2. Put two drops of mild dish soap in the water. Mix the soap and water together until the dish soap starts to sud. You can use dish soap on most materials like copper, stainless steel, aluminum, and non-stick pots and pans. Avoid washing cast iron with soap or it may affect the taste of your food.

3. Scrub the inside and outside of the pot or pan with a sponge. Let hot water and soap sit in the pot or pan for five minutes. Concentrate on spots that have stuck-on food or areas that are particularly dirty.

- Do not use abrasive sponges or steel wool to clean non-stick or stainless steel pots because you can scratch them.

4. Rinse the pot or pan with hot water. Hold the pot or pan under the faucet until you rinse away all the remaining soap suds. If you don't rinse your pots or pans thoroughly, your food may taste like soap.

5. Dry the pot and pan. Rub the inside and outside of the pot or pan with a rag until it's completely dry. You can also dry the pot or pan on a drying rack.

Method 2

Cleaning Copper Pots and Pans

1. Place the pot or pan in the sink and cover it in table salt. Pour enough salt on the inside and outside of the pot or pan so that there is a thin layer that covers the entire surface of the copper kitchenware. Table salt will act as an abrasive and will help you scrub problem areas on your pots and pans.

2. Pour white wine vinegar over the salt. Pour enough vinegar over the salt to wet down the pot or pan. Don't pour too much or you'll rinse away the salt. The acidity in the vinegar will start to break down the tarnished areas in the copper.

3. Let the vinegar and salt sit on the pot or pan for 30 seconds. As the solution sits on the pot or pan, you should see tarnish and stains start to fade away. If you don't have white wine vinegar, you can use fresh lemon juice as an alternative.

4. Scrub the pot or pan with a sponge soaked in white vinegar. Pour enough white vinegar onto a

sponge to fully saturate it. Take the sponge and scrub back and forth on the inside and outside of the pot, concentrating on especially dirty spots. As you do this, dirty and tarnished areas should start to become shiny.

- Sprinkle more salt on problem areas.

5. Rinse the pot or pan with hot water. Spray down the pot or pan under the faucet until there are no more traces of vinegar or salt on your copper kitchenware.

6. Dry the pot or pan with a rag. Rub over the inside and outside of the pan, making sure to pick up all the remaining moisture from the cookware.

Method 3

Cleaning Aluminum Pots and Pans

1. Pour three parts water to one part white wine vinegar into the pot or pan. Mix the solution with a spoon or a fork until it becomes well incorporated. The acidic vinegar will clean dirty and tarnished areas on the aluminum.

2. Bring the solution to a boil on the stove top. Turn your stovetop to high and bring the mixture to a boil. Let the solution boil for a minute. Your pot or pan should already start looking cleaner.

3. Add 2 tbsps (15.62 g) of baking soda to the pot or pan. Take the kitchenware off the heat and place it into your sink. Pour the baking soda into the pot or pan. It should start to fizz and react to the vinegar and water solution. Let the baking soda sit in the pot or pan until it stops fizzing, then pour it out into your sink.

4. Scour the pot or pan with a sponge. Use a non-abrasive sponge to scour the inside and outside of the pot or pan. Add more water and baking soda to especially troublesome areas until the pot or pan looks shiny.

5. Rinse the pot or pan. Hold the pot or pan under the sink and run hot water from the faucet. Continue rinsing it until all of the baking soda and vinegar solution is removed from the pot or pan.

6. Dry the pot or pan. Wipe down the inside and outside of the pot with a cotton rag or paper towels. Continue to wipe the kitchenware until it's completely dry.

Method 4

Cleaning Cast Iron Pots and Pans

1. Wash the pan with hot water and a sponge. Rub back and forth over the surface and interior of the pan. Take notice of places that have stuck on food. If you clean the cast iron immediately after using it, most foods will come off fairly easily.

- This method of cleaning should retain the seasoning on your cast iron skillet.

- Don't soak your cast iron or leave it in the sink or it may rust.

2. Scrub kosher salt into the pan. If there are areas on the pan that have stuck-on food, sprinkle some table or sea salt over the food and scrub it down with a sponge. The salt will act as an abrasive and will help remove the food from the pot or pan.

3. Rinse the pot or pan. Run the pan under your faucet and rinse all of the food particles off the pot or pan. If you notice that there's still stuck on food, sprinkle more salt and continue scrubbing.

4. Dry the pan thoroughly. Once the pot or pan is clean, use a cloth or rag to dry it. Remove all moisture from the cast iron before storing it.

Maintenance Operations: An Integrated Study

4

Outdoor maintenance operations in resorts, theme parks and hotels include pool management, fountain management, etc. Water in the swimming pool need to be filtered as well as treated chemically for eliminating waterborne diseases. The aspects elucidated in this chapter are of vital importance, and provide a better understanding of maintenance operations in the hospitality industry.

How to Maintain Swimming Pool

Having a swimming pool on property can be a pretty sweet deal during those hot summer months. But like most good things, a swimming pool requires quite a bit of maintenance and attention to detail. Many people choose to enlist the help of pool professionals, but if you're more of a do-it-yourself kind of person read on to find out how to keep the pool's water sparkling clean.

Part 1

Understanding Pool's Water Needs

1. Become familiar with pool's total alkalinity and pH levels. Total alkalinity is a way of measuring the water's ability to neutralize acidity. The water's alkalinity levels are directly related to The water's pH; the higher the total alkalinity, the higher the pH levels of the pool's water will be.

- pH levels measure how acidic or basic substances are. The pH scale has a range between 0 and 14, with a neutral pH at 7.

2. Know pool's chlorine, calcium hardness, cyanuric acid, and total dissolved solids levels. Besides the pH and alkaline levels, these are also important considerations. Make sure you understand what they are and how they benefit the water.

- Chlorine is used to disinfect and sanitize the water.

- Calcium hardness refers to the amount of calcium present in the water. If the calcium levels are too low the water will become corrosive, potentially ruining the body of the pool.

- Cyanuric acid protects the chlorine in the water from the sun's ultraviolet rays.

- Total dissolved solids are mainly composed of inorganic salts (calcium, magnesium, potassium, sodium, bicarbonates, chlorides and sulfates) and small amounts of other organic materials dissolved in the water.

3. Identify pool water's pH, total alkalinity, chlorine, cyanuric acid, calcium hardness, and total dissolved solids levels. Keep these recommended level ranges in mind.

- pH: 7.2 - 7.8

- Total alkalinity: 80 - 120 ppm

- Chlorine: 1.0 - 2.0 ppm

- Cyanuric Acid: 40 - 80 ppm

- Calcium hardness: 180 - 220 ppm, though some say 200 - 400

- Total Dissolved Solids: below 5000 ppm

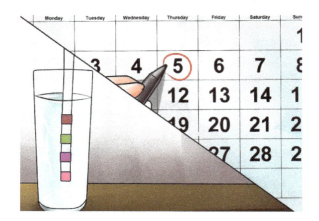

4. Know testing timelines for each water component. When you test the pool's water, you should observe certain timelines in order for pool to function well, and for the water to stay clean and healthy. Each element, like the pH for example, has to be tested at a specific point. Some professionals advise daily testing, which can be difficult for many people. Keep the following timeframes in mind to ensure proper pool functions:

- pH should be tested twice a week.
- Total alkalinity should be tested once a week, and at least once a month.
- Chlorine should be tested twice a week.
- Cyanuric acid should be tested twice a season.
- Calcium hardness should be tested twice a season.
- Total dissolved solids should be tested once a week, and at least once a month.

Part 2

Testing the Pool's Water

1. Purchase testing strips from the local pool store. Buy the strips that identify chlorine, alkaline, pH, and cyanuric acid. Nowadays, you don't have to bother with different tests for different chemicals.

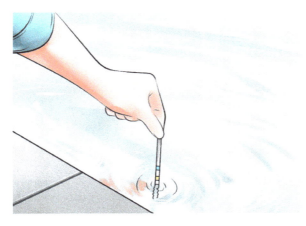

2. Dip the test strip into the pool. Move to an area that's separated from the pool's skimmer, and dip the test strip about 18 inches (46 cm) into the water for about ten seconds.

3. Wait until the different colors fill in. Match the color readings to the color description on the product box or bottle. Make sure to read the product's instructions carefully, as different manufacturers might have different procedures.

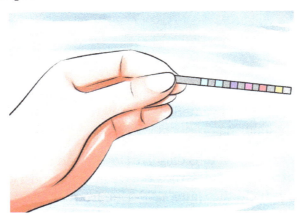

4. Make sure that the readings fall in the appropriate range. It's very important to adjust water in case readings do not match the recommended ranges. Using the right chemicals will easily adjust the ranges should they not meet suggested standards.

Part 3

Applying Chemicals to Pool

1. Have the right chemicals readily available. From time to time, you'll be faced with water problems that require aggressive chemical solutions. But generally, these chemicals should become part of pool maintenance routine as you might need to adjust certain levels sporadically. You product's instructions will provide appropriate dosage, should adjusting be necessary. Here are the most common chemicals you'll need:

- Chlorine
- Shocking products
- Algaecide

2. Apply chlorine to the pool. guests won't be too happy with algae and bacteria swimming alongside with you. Chlorine keeps these unwanted guests away. There are a few options out there when it comes to choosing the right chlorine products.

- Basic Chlorinating Tabs. These tabs dissolve slowly, and can be found in 1-inch and 3-inch sizes. They do a great job at keeping the pool clean. Plus, most chlorinating tablets contain a built-in stabilizer to shield the water's chlorine from the sun's rays. You can use the tablets in the floating dispenser, skimmer or automatic chlorinator.

- Liquid Chlorine. In liquid form, chlorine is quite similar to household bleach. But beware: it is also much stronger when it is designed for pools. Applying liquid chlorine is relatively easy, but it has a rather short shelf life. It won't last for more than a few weeks.

- Chlorinating Tabs. Some non-basic chlorinating tabs provide a multifunctional approach to pool maintenance; they sanitize the water while also shocking the pool. Shocking the pool gets rid of all sorts of contaminants.

- Chlorinating Granules. These granules come in multifunctional varieties that can help you resolve several issues at once; chlorinating, shocking and killing algae with a single, daily application.

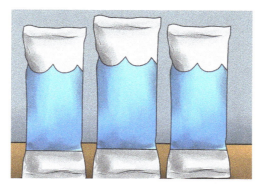

3. Shock the pool. Performing this task is crucial, as shocking keeps the water clear, and reduces eye irritation and odors coming from the chlorine. As mentioned, certain chlorine products already have built-in shockers, but if you choose to go with ones that do not, here are some shocking products that get the job done:

- Basic Shock Products. Basic products take care of killing bacteria, from breaking down cosmetic residue, suntan lotions, and any kind of swimmer waste. Using basic products to shock the water tone down chlorine.

- Multifunctional Shock Products. These products work fast and restore the water's clarity by eliminating all kinds of bacteria. Multifunctional products also balance the pool water's pH, boost filtration, and provide increased algae protection. The main pro is that these shocking products allow you to get back into the water within 15 minutes of use.

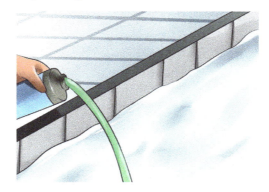

4. Add algaecide to the water. Just imagine, there are millions microscopic plants that can easily make the pool their home. Rain, wind, and fill water can allow these tiny forms of algae to settle into the pool, making the water quickly unusable and diminishing the efficiency of the pool chemicals. The filters will become quickly clogged, and the water's circulation will become sluggish. Algaecides effectively inhibit these small plants from invading the pool algae.

- Read the manufacturer's instructions carefully, and then pour the suggested amount of algaecides directly into the pool.

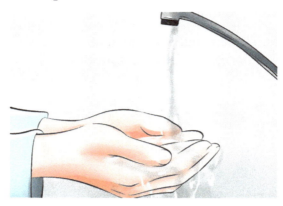

5. Handle necessary chemicals properly and carefully. There are many available, but they can be highly dangerous to humans and animals. Use caution when utilizing any chemical solution.

- Always wear rubber gloves.

- Wash hands immediately after being exposed to chemicals.

- Follow the dosage instructions carefully and store chemicals according to the manufacturer's directions.

- Never pour or return unused or wasted material to the original package, and do not throw it away in regular garbage.

- Do not light fires when using chemicals.

- Always add the chemical to the water, and not the other way around.

Part 4

Maintaining Pool's Filters

1. Manually clean pool daily, if possible. Use brushes, cleaners, and debris catching devices to remove surface dirt and excessive amounts of leaves or branches.

Maintenance Operations: An Integrated Study | 187

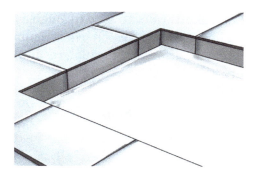

2. Keep pool's water between 1/3 and 1/2 way up the opening of the pool skimmer. This is the level at which pool operates best. A pool skimmer is a device that attracts the surface water of the pool. It pulls in small debris, like leaves and other things that might have fallen into the pool. A few inconvenient, and potentially damaging, things can happen if the water level is too high or too low for the skimmer.

- If the water level is too high, the water moves too slowly into the skimmer. This can result in debris bypassing the skimmer and accumulating in the pool.
- If the water level is too low, the skimmer is left with little to suck in and it can bottom out. It will suck in air instead, potentially burning the pool's motor pump.

3. Pour in water before backwashing and vacuuming. The action of vacuuming causes the water level to decrease, which is why you need to add water beforehand.

4. Be aware of different filtration systems. There are three basic filtration types:

- Sand filters: these filters are made of metal, fiberglass, or concrete and they contain a solid bed of specific sand. The sand does the job of trapping debris. Change the sand in the filter every five years.

- Cartridge filters: these filters allow water to seep through a fine filtrating surface. This filter keeps the impurities it catches until you clean it. An advantage of cartridge filters over sand ones, is that they have a greater surface area, which results in fewer clogs and easy maintenance. Replace them every 3-5 years.

- Diatomaceous earth filters: these filters contain porous bone material, which easily filters debris. Installing a DE filter is quite simple, as you place it directly into the skimmer. Backwashing and replacement/addition of a new DE has to be done once or twice a year.

5. Remember to maintain the filters. the pool filters are some of the most important tools for the pool, and need to stay very clean. So make sure to remember them in the pool care routine.

How to take Care of a Pool

Pool care can seem like an overwhelming task that you may outsource to the pros. Don't become intimidated by all the chemicals and test kits. Once you have all the supplies and follow a cleaning schedule, you'll find the task is manageable. Take pride in your pool and you'll feel better having cleaned the pool next time you're floating with a daiquiri.

Part 1

Getting the Equipment

1. Determine how to chlorinate. Chlorine is necessary for any pool owner, but there are a few options on how to administer the chlorine. You can administer chlorine manually or you can invest in

a salt water system that creates its own chlorine. Salt water pools are more expensive, but require less maintenance and use safer chlorine levels than regular pools.

- If you go with a salt water system, you can avoid doing much of what is discussed below.

2. Gather test equipment. A major aspect of proper pool care is how regularly you test the alkalinity, pH, calcium hardness, and chlorine. At all major pool supply stores you can buy basic and advanced testing equipment. The equipment consists of a container and a series of chemicals that respond to certain chemicals in the pool.

- The tests require you to add two-five drops of various chemicals and compare the color of your pool water to a chart. From this this information you'll know if your pool is safe to use.

- There are also test strips that use a similar color comparison test.

3. Buy a cleaner. All pools use a motorized pool cleaner and they come in three different types. Use the following information to decide on which is best for you and your pool:

- Suction side pool cleaners are low in cost, require fewer moving parts, and are easy to maintain. The only problem is they increase pressure on your filter and require a pool pump.

- Pressure side pool cleaners are similar to the suction cleaner expect they relieve pressure on the pool filter. The only problem with these is that they sometimes require an extra booster pump.

- Robotic cleaners offer superior cleaning, energy efficiency, and eliminates the wear on your pool. The only drawback to the robotic cleaners is that they are much more expensive.

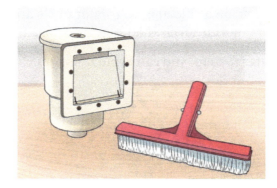

4. Gather a skimmer and brush. The skimmer and brush system accounts for all the blemishes not picked up by the pool cleaner. You can usually buy a kit at your pool supply store that includes a staff with an interchangeable skimmer or brush.

5. Buy chemicals. For your first time purchasing pool chemicals, go to a pool supply store and talk to a specialist. These are serious chemicals that could cause problems for your pool goers' health. Find an all inclusive starter kit that includes chlorine, calcium, alkalinity stabilizer, and algaecide.

- You can also substitute chlorine with bromine. Bromine tablets are reliable in killing bacteria and keeping your pool clear.

Part 2

Maintaining the Pool

1. Install your pool cleaner. You should plan on connecting your pool cleaner about once a week.

Doing this reduces the amount of chemicals you'll need to add to the pool. If your cleaner attaches to a pump, you'll need to attach the hose attached to the cleaner into the pump.

- The pump should be in your pool. It will be the spot in your pool that pumps out water.
- After each use, you should check and clean out the filter of the cleaner.

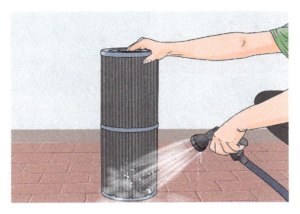

2. Clean the pool filter. There are three different types of filters: cartridge, sand, and diatomaceous earth. Each type of filter will require different cleaning techniques. For each filter you'll need to make sure the system is off and bleed all the air from the filter.

- For cartridge filters you'll need to remove the filter out its base and take time to spray down the cartridge with a hose. Use a high pressured hose with a point for best results.
- To clean a sand filter you'll need to make sure the sand filter is detached from the plumbing of the pool system. It's best to do this at the start of the season. Then take the time to clean out the top part of the filter with a high pressured hose.
- Diatomaceous earth filters should be cleaned once a month. The first step is to backwash the filter, then spend time spraying the grids with a high pressured hose.

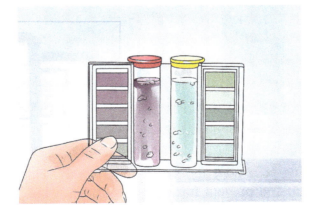

3. Balance the pool. About once a week you should use the chemical tester kit to ensure you have the proper chemical levels. Be sure you check the three main tests: pH, alkalinity, and calcium hardness. Use the color coded guide on your test kit to determine if you need more or less chemicals.

- Doing this regularly increases the longevity of your pool supplies and creates a safe space for your pool guests.

4. Chlorinate your pool. You will want your chlorine level to fall between 1 and 4 ppm for safe levels. You can use chlorine tabs which have a built-in stabilizer to protect your chlorine from sun burn-off. Liquid chlorine is easy to apply but will not last as long. The other option is to use the standard chlorine powder for an effective sweep of bacteria.

- Always follow the instructions listed on the product to ensure you don't over chlorinate your pool.

- Wear gloves and protective eyewear when handling chlorine. Even when using the tablets, you can still create skin irritation when handled raw.

5. Shock your pool. Shocking your pool should be done weekly. This can remove cloudy water, chlorine odor, eye irritation, and prevent future issues from arising. You can either use a basic shock or a multifunctional shock product. The basic shock products are limited in what they will kill and require an absence from the pool for longer than the multifunctional shock products.

- The largest difference is that the multifunctional shock product stabilizes the chemicals as well as cleans your pool fast.

6. Add algaecide. After a heavy rain, millions of microscopic plant organism can enter your pool and form algae. If you leave this problem unchecked your water could become unstable due to clogged filters, low water circulation, and a general reduced effectiveness of pool chemicals.

- There are preventive algaecides that work better for preventing algae and then there are fast working algaecides that wipe everything out quickly.

Part 3

Caring for the Pool Daily

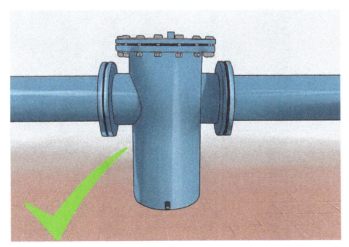

1. Check your baskets. Each pool will have at least one basket filter which collects small and large debris. It's important to check these more frequently because they are where dead rodents and frogs end up. Decomposing carcasses can seriously hinder your pools safety for swimmers.

- Use a hose and give the basket a good spray before returning to its base.

- If you found anything large, check the chemicals and shock your pool before returning for a dip.

2. Skim the surface. Skimming the surface of your pool every day can seem like a burden. If you care for the surface everyday, you will avoid spending a long time cleaning the surface.

- If left unattended for days, small bacteria can collect and attract water spiders. No kid likes swimming with spiders.

3. Brush the edges. If you look at your pool, you may not need to brush the sides everyday. Get into the habit of brushing the edges and bottom of the pool. Once you see dirt coming off the walls, direct the dirt, using your brush, to a filter.

4. Maintain a clean pool deck. If you have a dirty pool deck, you'll eventually have that mess in your pool. Take time to spot sweep your pool deck as needed.

How to Raise pH in Pool

Low pH levels in a pool can be caused by rainwater and other foreign particles getting into the water. Corrosion of metal accessories, burning of the nose and eyes, and itchy skin are signs of low pH levels in a pool. Regular testing and chemical treatment help maintain pH levels. Soda ash (or sodium carbonate) is the most common way to raise pH levels.

Part 1

Testing the Pool's pH

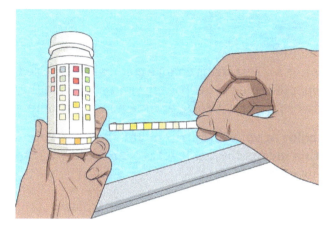

1. Test the pool water's pH level with test strips. Get pH testing strips at your local pool store, big-box store, or order them online. Follow the product's instructions, which are typically dipping the strip into the water and checking its color against the range listed on the product.

- Some pH test kits require you to fill a small tube with pool water and add drops which change color based on the pH.

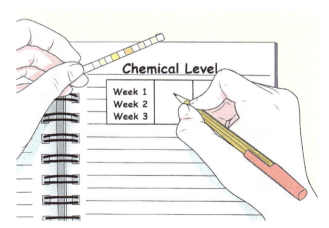

2. Check the chemical levels one to two times per week. Record the pH level in a small notebook to track the change over time. The pH of your pool changes frequently due to many causes. This is why it's important to check often. Write the pH down in a notebook to track it as it changes over time.

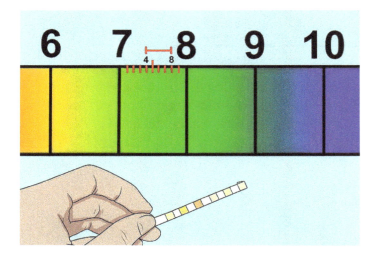

3. Aim for a pH level of 7.4 to 7.8.. Test strips change color when exposed to water. The color corresponds to the pH level. Match the color to the package and you'll find the current pH level. The ideal pH level for a pool is between 7.4 and 7.8. Determine how many points you need to raise the pH.

- For example, the color of your test strip might show the yellow of a banana. According to your product, this means the pH level is 7.2. You'd want to raise the pH by a minimum of .2 and a maximum of .6.

Part 2

Calculating the Soda Ash Needs

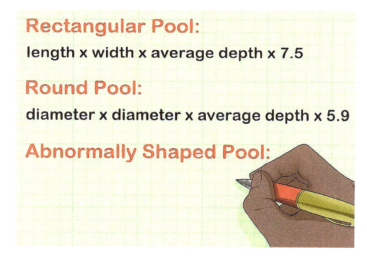

1. Calculate the number of gallons (liters) in your pool. If you already know how many gallons (liters) your pool holds, use that number. If you need to figure out the number of gallons (liters), you'll multiply the volume by a multiplier based on the shape of the pool. Use a measuring tape.

- For a rectangular pool, the formula is length X width X average depth X 7.5. If your pool has a deep end and a shallow end, measure the depth of each, add them, and divide by two to figure out the average depth.

- For a round pool, the formula is diameter X diameter X average depth X 5.9. If part of the pool is deeper, take the shallow depth plus the deeper depth and divide the number by two.

- For abnormally shaped pools, adjust these formulas to figure the gallons (liters) in each section, or ask a pool expert for an estimate on how many gallons (liters) your pool holds.

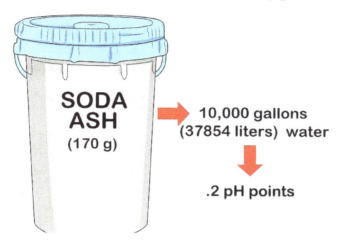

2. Figure out how much soda ash you need. Use about six ounces (170 g) of soda ash to raise 10,000 gallons (37854 liters) of water by .2 pH points. Start with this figure as a guide, and add more soda ash later if you need to raise the pH by more.

- For example, you test the pH of the water and it shows 7.2. You want to raise it to 7.6. Your pool holds exactly 10,000 gallons (37854 liters) of water. Use 12 ounces (340 g) of soda ash for the first round.

3. Buy the soda ash at a pool store or order it online. Soda ash may be labeled by many different manufacturer names. Look at the ingredients of the product and make sure sodium carbonate is the active ingredient. If you aren't sure what to buy, ask an employee which products contain soda ash.

- If you don't have a pool store near you, check at a water treatment store, hardware store, or big-box store like Walmart.

Part 3
Adding Soda Ash to the Pool

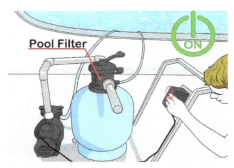

1. Leave the pool filter on while you add the soda ash. Soda ash works best when it can circulate throughout the pool. To make sure this happens, run the pool filter on its regular circulation setting. If you've turned the filter off to clean the pool, turn it back on.

2. Get a five gallon (19 liter) bucket and fill it with water. You don't want to throw the soda ash directly into the pool because it won't mix in evenly enough. Instead, dissolve it into water and spread that into the pool. If you don't have a five gallon bucket, any bucket will work. Mix the soda ash into at least one gallon (3.8 L) of water.

- It's important to fill the bucket first and add the soda ash second.

3. Measure the soda ash into the bucket of water. Measure out the soda ash you need based on the amounts described above. Use a basic kitchen measuring cup or a scale to measure out the amount you need. Pour the soda ash into the bucket of water.

- Remember, don't put the soda ash into the bucket before the water.

Maintenance Operations: An Integrated Study | 199

4. Pour the soda ash water around the pool. For in-ground pools, walk around the perimeter, slowly pouring the water from the bucket into the pool. For above ground pools, pour it around the edge of the pool as best you can.

- If you want, use an old plastic cup to scoop water out of the bucket and toss a cupful at a time into the pool.

5. Check the pH of the water after one hour. Give the soda ash time to circulate throughout the pool and alter the pH of the water. After one hour, grab another test strip and dip it into the water. See if the pH is in the range you need it to be.

6. Add more soda ash as needed. You generally don't want to add more than one pound (454 g) total of soda ash per 10,000 gallons (37854 liters) of water. If you add more than that, the water starts to become cloudy.

- If the pH isn't where you want it to be, check it in a day or two and add more soda ash in the quantities you already figured.

How to Eliminate and Prevent Green Algae in a Swimming Pool

Green water or floating algae are common problems in swimming pools. Treatment can take multiple chemicals and several days of waiting if the algae has had time to build up. You can prevent the algae from returning with much less effort through regular pool maintenance.

Method 1

Killing Green Algae with Chlorine

1. Use chlorine as your go-to algae killer. When your pool water is green or contains visible algae clumps, your pool does not have enough chlorine. "Shocking" the pool with a large dose of chlorine is the most effective way to kill the existing algae and bring your pool back to sanitary conditions. This usually works within 1–3 days, but can take up to a week if pool conditions are poor.

- The other methods listed below are faster, but may not fix underlying sanitation concerns. They are also more expensive and can have unwanted side effects.

2. Brush the walls and floor of the swimming pool. Brush vigorously to remove as much of the algae as possible. This will reduce the amount of time it takes to kill and clear the algae bloom. Pay special attention to the steps, behind ladders, and other nooks and crannies where algae tends to gather.

- Make sure the brush is compatible with your pool. Steel brushes work well on concrete, while nylon brushes are preferable for vinyl pools.

3. Review pool chemical safety. You'll be handling dangerous chemicals during this method. Always read the safety information on the labels first. At minimum, follow these safety standards for all pool chemicals:

- Wear gloves, eye protection, and clothing that covers your skin. After use, wash hands and inspect clothes for chemicals.

- Avoid inhaling the chemicals. Use caution when handling in windy weather.

- Always add chemicals to water, never water to chemicals. Do not place wet scoops back in container.

- Store chemicals in sealed, fireproof containers, away from children, on separate shelves on the same level (not one above the other). Many pool chemicals explode when they touch another pool chemical.

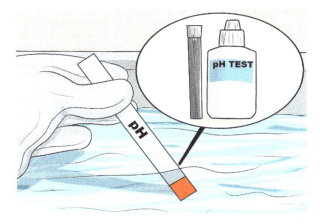

4. Adjust the pool pH. Use a swimming pool pH test kit to measure the pH of your water. If the pH is above 7.6 — which is common during an algae bloom — add a pH reducer (such as sodium bisulfate) to your pool according to label instructions. Aim for pH levels between 7.2 and 7.6 to make your chlorine more effective and reduce the growth of the infestation. Wait at least a couple hours, then test the pool again.

- Test kits that use tablets or droppers are much more accurate than paper test strips.

- If pH levels are back to normal but total alkalinity is above 120 ppm, check the pH reducer label for instructions to bring total alkalinity down between 80 and 120 ppm.

5. Choose a chlorine shock product. The chlorine you use for regular pool treatment may not be the best choice for a shock treatment. Ideally, you should use a liquid chlorine product intended for swimming pools. The product should contain sodium hypochlorite, calcium hypochlorite, or lithium hypochlorite.

- Avoid calcium hypochlorite if you have hard water.

- All hypochlorite products are flammable and explosive. Lithium is relatively safer, but much more expensive.

- Avoid granular or tablet chlorine products (such as dichlor or trichlor), which contain stabilizers that should not be added to the pool in large quantities.

6. Add an extra large dose of shock. Check your chlorine product's label for "shock" instructions. To fight algae, use twice the recommended amount for a regular shock. Use triple the amount if the water is very murky, or even quadruple if you can't even see the top rung of the ladder. With the pool filter running, add the shock directly to the perimeter of the pool. (If you have a vinyl pool liner, pour the shock into a bucket of pool water first to avoid bleaching.)

- Warning — liquid chlorine will explode and produce corrosive gas if it touches chlorine tablets or granules. Never pour the liquid chlorine into your pool skimmer or anything that contains these products.

- Because UV rays in sunlight break down chlorine, shocking is most effective when added in the evening and left overnight.

7. Test the pool again the next day. After the pool filter has been running for 12–24 hours, examine the pool. Dead algae turns white or gray, and either suspends in the pool water or settles to the floor. Whether or not the algae is dead, test the pool again for the new chlorine and pH levels.

- If your chlorine levels are higher (2–5 ppm) but the algae is still there, keep maintaining these levels as usual for the next couple days.

- If chlorine levels have risen but are still below 2ppm, shock a second time the next evening.

- If there was no significant change in your chlorine levels, your pool likely has too much cyanuric acid (more than 50 ppm). This comes from using granulated or tablet chlorine, and can "lock" your chlorine into unusable forms. The only way to fight this is to shock repeatedly (sometimes many times), or to partially drain your pool.

- Large amounts of leaf litter or other objects in the pool can also eat up your chlorine. If the pool has been unused a long time, this could take a full week and several shock treatments.

8. Brush and test daily. Brush vigorously to fight new algal growth on the walls. Over the next couple days, the chlorine should kill the algae. Test daily to confirm that chlorine and pH levels are acceptable.

- A well maintained pool has roughly the following values: Free Chlorine: 2-4 ppm, pH: 7.2 – 7.6, Alkalinity: 80 – 120 ppm and Calcium Hardness: 200 – 400 ppm. Slight differences in standards are common, so a small deviation should not be an issue.

9. Vacuum the dead algae. Once there is no green color left in your pool, vacuum up all the dead algae until the water is clear. You may skip this step and let the filter handle it, but only if you have a powerful filter and are willing to wait several days.

- If you're having trouble getting all the algae, add coagulant or flocculant so it clumps together. These are available at pool stores.

10. Clean the filter. If you have a D.E. filter, set it to backwash. If you have a cartridge filter, remove it and clean the cartridge with a hose at high pressure, followed by dilute muriatic acid or liquid chlorine if necessary. If you do not clean the filter thoroughly, dead algae may block the filter.

Method 2
Other Green Algae Treatments

1. **Improve circulation to handle small spots of algae.** If small clumps of algae form but do not spread to the rest of the pool, you may have areas of stagnant water. Check that your water jets are functioning properly. They should point into the water at an angle, so the water moves in a spiral pattern.

2. **Gather the algae with a flocculant.** A flocculant or coagulant clumps the algae together, making it possible to vacuum living algae. This may take a hard day of work, but your pool should be clear by the end of it. This is the fastest way to get your pool looking good, but it does *not* make the water safe to swim in. If algae can multiply, so can viruses and bacteria. Follow this with a chlorine shock treatment to sanitize the pool, and do not swim in the pool until chlorine and pH levels are back to normal.

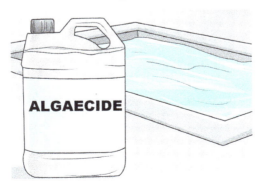

3. **Treat the pool with algaecide.** Algaecide will certainly kill your algae, but the side effects and expense may not be worth it. Here are a few factors to weigh when considering this option:

- Some algaecide products are not powerful enough to treat an existing bloom, especially if you have black algae as well. Ask a pool store employee for help, or find a product with 30%+ active ingredients.

- Quaternary ammonia algaecides ("poly quats") are cheap, but cause your water to foam. Many people find this annoying.

- Copper-based algaecides are more effective, but expensive. They usually stain your pool walls as well.

- After adding the algaecide, wait at least 24 hours before adding other chemicals.

Method 3
Preventing Algae

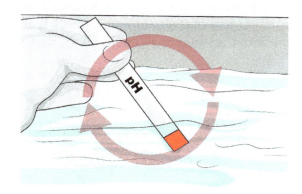

1. Maintain your pool water. Algae should not grow if you keep on top of your pool chemistry. Test the pool regularly for free chlorine levels, pH, alkalines, and cyanuric acid. The faster you catch a problem, the easier it will be to deal with it.

- Daily testing is ideal, especially in the week or two following an algal bloom. Always test at least twice a week during the swimming season.

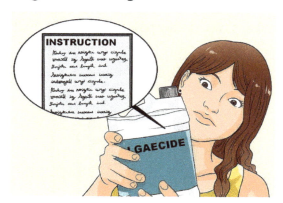

2. Add an algaecide as a preventative. Algaecides are best used in small, weekly doses when pool conditions are normal. This will kill algae populations before they have a chance to grow. Check the product label for instructions.

- Make sure to follow instructions for regular prevention, not for existing algae blooms. Too much algaecide may stain your pool or cause foaming.

3. Remove phosphates. Algae feed off several nutrients in the water, notably phosphates. Phosphate test kits are a cheap way to test for these chemicals in your pool. If they are present, use a commercial strength phosphate remover from a pool supply store. Let the filter and robot or manual vacuum remove the phosphate remover over the next day or two. Shock the pool once the phosphates are at a reasonable level.

- Pool professionals disagree over acceptable phosphate levels. 300 ppm is probably low enough unless you have recurring algae problems.

How to Vacuum Pool and Backwash the Filter

This article attempts to explain the steps required to vacuum out a pool. There are different kinds of filtration systems for pools, such as cartridge filters, sand filters, and diatomaceous earth (D.E.) filters. The instructions here assume that you are using either a sand filter or D.E. filter, though some cartridge-based systems may be similar.

Steps

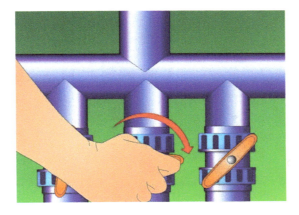

1. Turn off skimmers as noted on pipes.

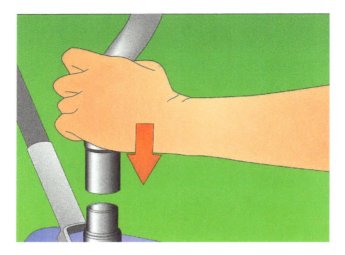

2. Start by attaching the vacuum hose to the vacuum head.

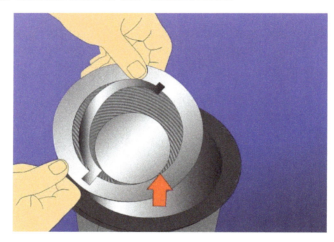

3. Flood hose with water before placing adapter in skimmer to avoid loss of prime. Some skimmers require you to remove the basket before you can attach the hose, so be sure to do this if necessary. Holding one end of the vacuum line over the return port is a good way to bleed out the air trapped in the line.

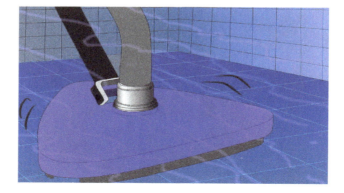

4. Vacuum per manufacturer instructions. Basically, move very slowly and methodically while vacuuming. Follow a grid pattern to ensure all areas of the floor and slopes are cleaned.

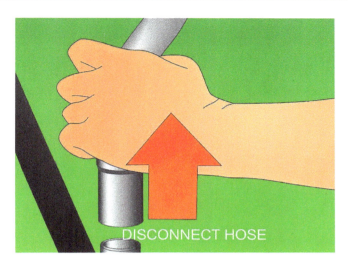

5. Disconnect the hose from the skimmer and remove vacuum equipment.

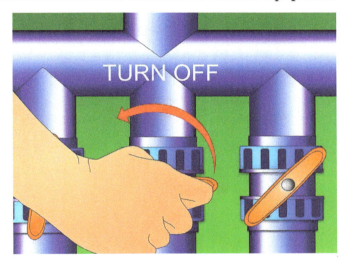

6. Turn off the pump.

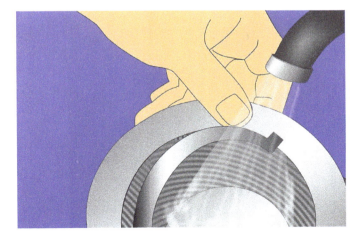

7. Clean the skimmer basket and hair basket. The hair basket is the one located at the pump.

8. Turn filter handle to the "BACKWASH" setting, and then turn on the pump.

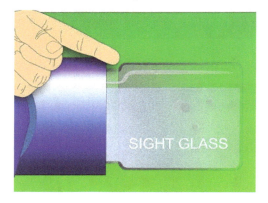

9. Continue to let the pump run until the water in the sight glass on the filter is clear.

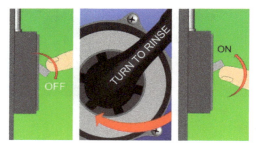

10. Turn off the pump and set filter handle to "RINSE", and then turn on the pump for about 60 seconds.

11. Turn off the pump and return the filter handle to "FILTER".

Maintenance Operations: An Integrated Study | 211

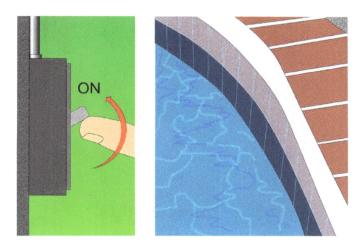

12. Turn on pump and resume normal use of the pool.

How to Drain and Refill Swimming Pool

Swimming pool water can get bad over the years — so bad that chemicals lose their effectiveness. With this information and a free weekend, you (and a friend) can drain and refill the pool without spending much more than $200 (not including necessary chemicals for new water).

Part 1

Draining

1. Go to an improvement store and rent a submersible sump pump. Sump pumps can be rented for about $36/24 hours. Do this early in the day so the pool is empty before dark.

- The rental should include rubber fire hoses in 50 feet (15.2 m) lengths. Two should be enough for most hotelowner, but check to make sure the pool is not more than 100 feet (30.5 m) from the clean out/sewer access point.

2. Set up the sump pump and discharge hoses, connecting the hoses to a clean out. This step is very important. Most municipalities won't let you drain the water directly into the street or a neighbor's yard, for example. That leaves you two options of where to drain the water:

- Directly into the clean out. This is usually a 3 to 4 inch (7.6 to 10.2 cm) plastic pipe on the property, usually outside a bathroom or the kitchen, with a screw cap on it which leads directly into the sewer. The city will reuse this water. On older hotels, one clean out usually exists and is elevated on a wall. On newer hotels, two clean outs usually exist, and they are ground-level — sometimes obscured by landscaping.
    - o Using a clean connected to a wall is risky and could cause water damage to the house. If the clean out is connected directly to house. Consult a pool specialist or general contractor before proceeding.
- Irrigate the lawn, plants, or other shrubbery. This is not recommended if you are draining the entire pool, nor is it a great idea on certain lawns or plants that don't react well to excessive salt or chlorine. Certain grasses and Oleander species can take pool water, but citrus, hibiscus, or other salt-sensitive plants should not be irrigated in this fashion.

3. Lower the pump into the pool and plug it in. Make sure the hose is properly attached and make sure the other end of the hose is stuck into the clean out before plugging in the pump. Some hoses will go down about 3 feet (0.9 m) into the clean out before hitting something; make sure to lodge it in properly.

Maintenance Operations: An Integrated Study | 213

4. Watch the water disappear, monitoring the discharge carefully. The time it takes to drain the pool water will depend on the municipality laws, the pump speed, and the total size of the pool.

- Although it may sound strange, check the municipality's laws concerning the discharge rate. In some municipalities, the discharge rate is capped quite low — Phoenix, for example, sets theirs at 12 gallons (45.4 L) per minute (or 720 gal/hr). This ensures safe disposal of the water into the sewer.

- Most good pumps will far exceed the municipality's maximum discharge rate. They'll function safely at 50 gallons/minute, and top out at about 70 gallons/minute.

- The pool size will also determine how long it takes. If you're pumping at 30 gallons/minute, or 1,800 gallons/hour, and you have a 25,000 gallon (94,635.3 L) pool, it will take roughly 14 hours to drain the pool.

5. Every foot or so of water level decrease, spray the perimeter of the pool's previous water line with a hose. Do this especially if the water is dirty, as this will save you time in the end. Try some brushing while you are at it.

6. Wait as the pump removes almost all of the water, draining the last bit manually. How much

water the pump is able to remove will depending on the pool's contours at the deep end. Drain the last foot or so manually with two buckets. This is where a helper comes in handy.

Part 2
Cleaning

1. Blast debris out of the pop-ups with the hose. If you have an in-floor cleaning system, this is a great option for you to use. Alternately, you can contact the manufacturer of the pool for specific servicing/repair tips.

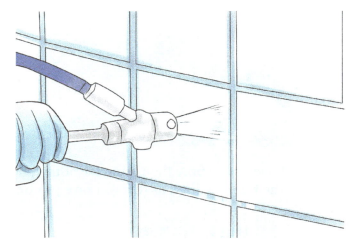

2. Clean away any calcium or scale rings. Now is also a good time to clean away calcium or scale rings (if any exist). Calcium, Lime, and Rust remover, also known as CLR, usually works pretty well. Work at the tougher buildups with a putty knife, being careful not to damage the lining of the pool. Lesser buildups can usually be dispatched with rubber gloves, a scrubbing pad, and the aforementioned CLR.

- To keep the rings from reappearing, you can buy some "stain and scale inhibitor." Check the manufacturer's instructions for applications, as well as for repetitions. Some inhibitors need to be reapplied every month to be effective.

3. Perform an acid wash on the pool (optional). A good acid wash will clean the walls of pool, keep the water looking bright and transparent, and make the whole shebang an altogether more pleasant experience. If the pool is already fairly clean or you don't have time, you may skip this step.

Part 3
Refilling

1. Estimate the amount of time it will take to fill the pool with the current pumps. You don't want to go to sleep and wake up with a lake in the backyard. Do a little bit of homework to avoid needing to damage-control in the end.

2. Fill up the pool. Connect one or more garden hoses to available spigots and drop them into the

side of the pool. Turn them on. If the pool was newly plastered for example, you probably want to tie on some socks to the spout of the hose and secure with a couple rubber bands. That way, the force of the water doesn't mess with the plaster.

- Water should not be expensive. If you need to, call the city and inquire about how much they charge.

3. Wait for the water to settle a few hours before adding any chemicals or additives. You're almost there. All you need to do now is test the alkalinity of the water, pH, and calcium hardness. After you've performed these tests, adjust the alkalinity, pH, and hardness of the water appropriately before adding chlorine, CYA (Cyanuric Acid), or salt.

How to Clean a Water Fountain

Water fountains come in all shapes and sizes, from decorative water fountains to drinking fountains. Cleaning these fountains mostly involves scrubbing them down and making sure to remove any hard water buildup. While decorative fountains only need to be cleaned every month or so, drinking fountains should be cleaned at least once a day to keep them sanitary.

Method 1

Washing a Decorative Water Fountain

1. Turn off the fountain. Before cleaning your fountain, it's best to turn it off and take the pump out to make cleaning easier. You can also remove any items in the fountain, such as large rocks.

- Always check your manual before cleaning, as different fountains may require different cleaning methods.

2. Drain the water out of the fountain. For smaller fountains, you can just dump the water out. For larger fountains, a shop vac may be easier to remove the water from the fountain.

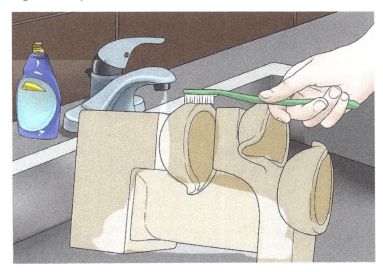

3. Scrub the fountain. If the fountain is small, it may be easiest to bring it into a sink to clean. If it's larger, you'll need to clean it outside. A toothbrush or other soft brush is perfect for this purpose. Use a mild soap such as dishwashing soap or even CLR to clean the fountain.

- If your fountain is copper, make sure you only use a very soft rag on it.

- Keep going until the fountain is clean. If you are having trouble removing algae, you can buy products specifically made for breaking down algae. Consider wiping the fountain down with a mild bleach solution to help keep new growth from happening.

- Clean smaller fountains more often (once a month) and larger fountains less often (every other month or so).

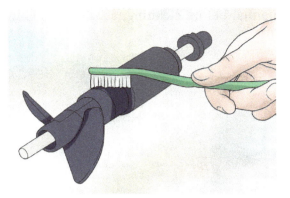

4. Clean the pump. In a sink, unscrew the side of the pump that comes off, which should show you the propeller. You can use the same brush you used on the fountain to clean the propeller. Get all the debris out you can, and then replace the pump in the fountain.

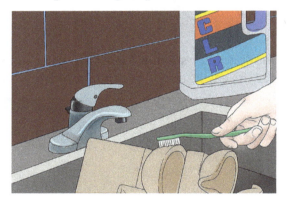

5. Descale the fountain. If your fountain has hard water buildup, use a special product to help remove it, such as CLR. You can also use a mixture of half white vinegar, half water. Let the fountain soak in the solution, and then scrub it again with a gentle brush or sponge.

Method 2

Cleaning a Drinking Fountain

1. See if the water is flowing freely. The water should flow out of the mouthpiece readily, and it

should lift up at least 3 inches above the fountain. The height of the stream is important because it keeps people from putting their mouths on the metal part of the fountain.

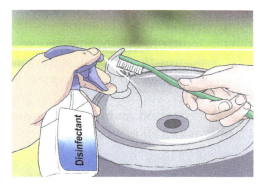

2. Clean the mouthpiece. Squirt disinfectant on the mouthpiece, as well as the guard that sits over it. Use a brush to clean all around the mouthpiece and guard, including where the water comes out. Once done, use water to rinse the area thoroughly.

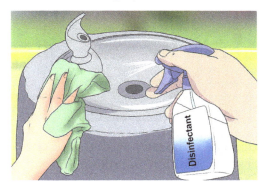

3. Wash the rest of the fountain. A damp cloth is generally enough to clean the rest of the fountain's surfaces. Wipe it down thoroughly. However, you may want to use some disinfectant on the areas that are most touched, such as the fountain's buttons. Wipe down areas you use disinfectant on with a clean cloth and water.

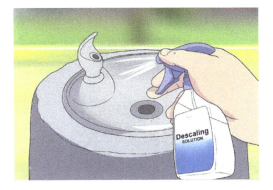

4. Descale the fountain. Drinking fountains need to be descaled from time to time because of a build up of hard water. Spray the fountain with a descaling solution where the it has hard water buildup, and then scrub it with a cloth soaked in the same solution until the scaling comes off. Wipe it down with clean water when you're done.

How to Maintain Indoor Fountains

Your indoor fountain can be kept in clean, optimal condition when you take steps to maintain your fountain on a routine basis. Although indoor fountains may be exposed to fewer natural elements, they can still develop algae and bacterial growth or experience low water levels due to evaporation. In addition to performing general maintenance on your indoor fountain, you must also clean the inside of your fountain and the pump at least once per month to prevent algae and mineral deposits from forming. With regular, proper care and maintenance, you can maintain the functionality and appearance of your indoor fountain and all its working components.

Method 1
General Maintenance

1. Keep your fountain pump submerged in water at all times. This will help circulate the water in your fountain and keep it filtered, in addition to minimizing the growth of algae. Your fountain pump may also become dry and burn out if it is not submerged in water consistently.

- Examine the water level around your fountain pump on a daily basis. This will allow you to become familiar with how often you need to add water to the fountain.

- Add water to your fountain as needed. This factor will vary depending on the indoor climate in which the fountain is located. For example, if the fountain resides in a warm, dry indoor climate, you may need to add water to the fountain on a daily basis.

2. Keep your fountain pump powered on constantly. This will help keep your fountain water clean and prolong the life of your pump; as turning the power off and on continually may cause the motor in the pump to wear at a faster pace.

- Ask a friend or family member to help maintain the water level in your fountain when you need to travel. This will prevent you from having to power off the fountain completely.

3. Use distilled water in your water fountain. Using distilled water is a natural way to keep your fountain clean and prevent algae growth; whereas tap water may contain minerals or other metals that can solidify and build up on the walls of your fountain and the pump.

Method 2
Cleaning Procedure

1. Turn off and unplug your fountain. This will eliminate your risk of electrical shock as you clean the fountain.

2. Remove any stones or pebbles from the inside of your fountain. Stones will need to be cleaned before they are placed back into the fresh water.

3. Remove the fountain pump from the fountain.

   - Consult your fountain's manual or contact the manufacturer directly if you are unsure how to remove the pump safely from the fountain.

4. Remove the water from your fountain. Depending on the size of your fountain, you can either empty the fountain over a sink or use a shop-vac to remove the water.

5. Clean your fountain and its components.

   - Use a soft, non-abrasive sponge to avoid scratching or damaging the fountain's interior and working parts.

   - Clean the fountain, pump, and stones using a cleaning mixture of warm water and mild liquid soap, or use a commercial calcium lime removal product. For an all-natural alternative, spray distilled white vinegar on the fountain's interior and parts, then scrub using a wet sponge.

- Use a toothbrush to clean any small, tough corners or spots that are hard to penetrate or reach with the sponge.

- Use a soft, clean rag or cloth to dry and remove any excess cleaning mixture from the fountain's interior and parts.

6. Place the fountain pump and stones back into the fountain.

7. Refill your fountain with fresh, clean water. The procedure for refilling your fountain will vary depending on its size.

- Pour bottled, distilled water into your fountain or use tap water from a sink. Depending on the size of your fountain, you can refill the fountain from the inside of a sink or use a bucket to transport the water from the sink over to the fountain.

8. Plug in your indoor fountain and power the fountain on.

- Observe the fountain for a few minutes to make sure the pump is properly re-installed, and that the fountain work efficiently.

How to Maintain Outdoor Fountains

An outdoor fountain adds beauty and ambiance to your yard and requires only occasional care. To keep your fountain running efficiently, you'll need to know basic maintenance procedures and have certain supplies on hand. If you want to know how to maintain outdoor fountains, follow these guidelines.

Steps

1. Examine the fountain for signs of wear. Because your fountain is out in the elements all day, it's going to suffer the effects of Mother Nature. Dirt, wind, animals and precipitation all can affect your fountain's operation, so it's important to make frequent checks to ensure it's running properly.

2. Keep your outdoor fountain's pump in good working order. The pump is the single most important piece of equipment in your fountain. If it's not working or working at reduced capacity, shut it off and remove it before making repairs. Look for obstructions and other signs of wear about once a month.

- Remove leaves and other debris from the pump's intake valve and housing. With the pump taken out of the fountain, wipe it clean with a damp cloth. Use a toothbrush to scrub hard-to-reach areas.

- Flush the pump and hose lines if they appear to be clogged.
- Replace filters or damaged components as necessary.

3. Scrub the surface area of the fountain. Outdoor fountains can be dirtied by a variety of factors. Algae blooms, animal waste and mineral deposits can foul the water in your fountain and affect its appearance. Take steps to neutralize these conditions.

- Algae: The tiny organism can flourish in outdoor fountains, particularly in direct sunlight during the peak summer months. Gently scrub it away with a diluted bleach mixture. Thoroughly rinse the fountain afterward. You also can add all-natural products to the water to keep algae in check. These items are rich in enzymes that inhibit algae growth but do no harm pets or other animals.

- Animal waste: Birds are frequent visitors to outdoor fountains, and while they're often bright additions to the landscape, they can be messy. Wipe bird droppings away with a damp sponge but try not to use soap. Consider replacing the water, too.

- Mineral deposits: Hard-water stains often appear on the fountain surface as crusty, white buildups. Scrub these off with white vinegar and allow the fountain wash the deposits away.

4. Replenish the water in your fountain regularly. Experts suggest changing the water in an outdoor fountain at least once a week. Mix in additives designed to inhibit algae growth and deposit buildups with each water change. Fresh water helps keep the system running smoothly and makes the fountain inviting to wildlife.

Security Operations in Hotel 5

Guests need to feel relaxed and comfortable and safety becomes a key aspect of hotel management. Security guards, video surveillance, smoke detectors, adequate lighting are important measures that can be taken to prevent harm to the guests. This chapter discusses the methods of hotel security operations in a critical manner providing key analysis to the subject matter.

How to choose the Right Location for your Outdoor Security IP Camera

If a Network based IP or Analog camera is to be exposed to outdoor elements or is placed in an industrial setting, an external housing is need to protect it. There are standards that specify the degree of protection to be provided by enclosures. Two digits prefixed by the letters IP define the rating of protection look for IP 66 or higher. Vandalism and theft of hardware is not consider in this rating scheme.

Method 1

Environmental Factors

1. Camera housings are normally made of aluminum or more recently now from extremely durable specialty thermoplastics. Weather conditions, outdoor temperature and equipment temperature rating should dictate if the camera housings will require a heater, de icing system, multiple hi flow fans or possibly an active cooling system. Remember sensitive electronics are just that sensitive -long life, reliability and down time should be all be considered.

2. In climates where the weather can vary from bright sunlight to cold and damp there will need to be some form of heater mounted below the front glass plate or lower dome. The heater and fans act as a defogger for the lens and prevents the build up of condensation along it is suggested that a silica desiccant pack be placed in the housing. Dome housings, speed dome or dome enclosures are used for Pan Tilt and Zoom cameras because the internal mechanisms can be of a lighter construction and therefore permit very fast speeds of pan and tilt. If the dome is tinted or "smoked" it makes it difficult for a person to detect in which direction the camera is pointing.

3. All material in front of the camera lens will attenuate the light and an allowance of at least one full f-stop should be used in calculating lighting and camera sensitivity. An auto iris lens should always be used with an outdoor camera. This will give the camera a better dynamic range and protect the image sensor from being damaged by direct sunlight.

4. If you mount a camera behind glass, for example in an outdoor housing, make sure that the lens is close to the external lens. If it is too far away, reflections from the camera and the background may appear in the image.

Method 2
Lighting

1. If cameras are to be used at night additional external light sources may be required such as incandescent, HID or IR illumination.

2. Lamps should be mounted in such a way as to avoid reflections and shadows. Special color corrected lamps are available which produce a balanced white light suitable for most cameras.

3. Infrared illuminators can also be used for covert or semi-covert operation. Not all color cameras are rated for IR infrared illumination due to a lack of IR cut filter.

Method 3
Avoid Direct Sunlight

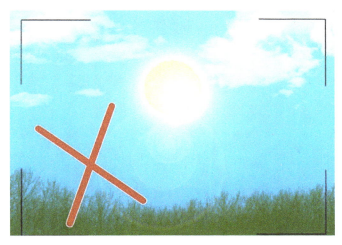

1. Always try to avoid direct sunlight in an image. Direct sunlight may "blind" the camera and filters and burn the CCD causing stripes in the image.

2. When using a camera outdoors, avoid including too much sky in the image. Due to the large contrast, the camera will adjust in order to achieve a good level for the sky and the interesting landscape or objects may appear too dark. One way to avoid these problems is to mount the camera high above the ground. Used a proper pole with sturdy pole mount adapter or wall mounted bracket and always use proper mountings to avoid vibrations caused by wind.

How to Install a Security Camera System for a Hotel

The idea of drilling holes through the walls of the hotel to run video and power cables for a security camera system might seem daunting, but many security systems come in all-included packages that make setting up your surveillance system a breeze.

Method 1
Preparing the Hotel

1. Make a diagram of your surveillance needs. It is both expensive and inefficient to monitor every square inch of your hotel, so you need to prioritize what areas you want to watch the most. Draw up a rough diagram of your hotel or print out the blueprints and note where you might want to place cameras. When you are done, check out each location to make sure it is not blocked by anything and provides the best view possible. You may want cameras for:

- Front and back doors.
- Off-Street Windows
- Large common spaces (kitchen, living room etc.)
- Driveways
- Porches
- Stairways

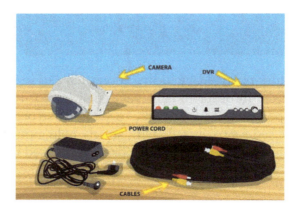

2. Buy the right package to suit your needs. You can buy each piece individually, but it is generally cheaper and easier to buy bundled security systems. At a minimum your system should have 1-3 cameras, a DVR (digital video recorder), appropriate wiring (siamese and BNC cables), and power cords. Unless you are choosing to monitor a large area, wireless cameras with wall mounting should cover your needs.

- Basic Security: Get a package with 2-3 outdoor cameras (to monitor doors), and a DVR with at least 3 days of recording time.

- Monitoring Valuables/Young Children: 1-3 indoor wireless cameras can cover a small room effectively and stream the footage right to your computer.

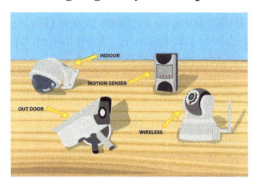

3. Alternatively, buy your cameras individually. Once you know how many cameras you need, you'll need to think about what specific cameras you want. A surveillance system can cost anywhere from a few hundred dollars to well over a thousand, so make sure you consider the type of cameras you need before buying -- the features below should be clearly labeled on the box. While you can buy all of the parts separately, buying a full "surveillance set" is usually cheaper and easier to install.

- Wireless vs. Wired: Wireless cameras are easy to set-up without drilling or running cables, but the quality can be sub-par the further they get away from the receiver. If you are covering a big area, go wired, but most hotel find wireless and easier set-up process.

- Indoor or Outdoor: Cameras that are not made to be placed outside will quickly break when exposed to rain and humidity, so be sure to choose accordingly.

- Motion Sensing: Some cameras will only record when they notice motion, saving lots of space and energy while only capturing footage when someone is in the room.

- Remote Viewing: Many high-end cameras offer the ability to stream their footage to your phone or laptop anywhere in the world, making it possible to check out the hotel through a provided program or app.

4. Set up a recording device and monitor. In order to store and view your footage, you need a Digital Video Recorder (DVR). This device receives all of the video feeds and broadcasts them onto a

monitor, usually a computer screen or small TV. DVRs have a variety of memory capacities that allow them to store a certain amount of video, from hundreds of hours to one day's worth of footage.

- If you buy a complete surveillance set the DVR is usually included with the camera.
- Network Video Recorders (NVR) and analog recorders (VCRs), also available for purchase, work the same way as a DVR, using an internet signal (NVR) or blank tapes (VCR) to record instead of a digital hard-drive. The following installation tips will work here as well.

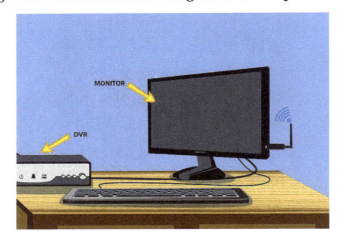

5. Test your equipment before installing. Make sure your cables, DVR, cameras, and monitor all work by connecting each one before you install anything.

Method 2

Installing a Camera

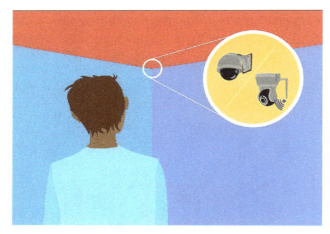

1. Choose a high, broad angle for your camera. The best angle of any room is usually looking down from the corner where the ceiling meets the walls. Make sure you can clearly see all entries and exits and that the camera is near a power outlet.

- If you are mounting a camera outside, place it above 10ft so that it cannot be easily knocked down.

Security Operations in Hotel | 233

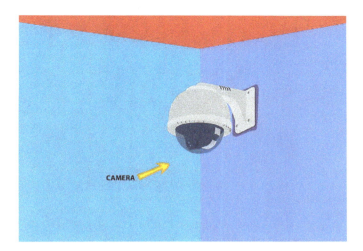

2. Mount your camera to the wall. Some cameras come with sticky pads to adhere your camera to the wall, but screwing your camera in is the safest way to mount your cameras long-term. While every camera is different, most of them can be mounted the same way:

- Place the mount in its desired location.
- Using a sharpie, make marks on the wall where each screw should go.
- Drill a hole for each screw using an electric drill
- Hammer in any molding pins.
- Screw the mount into the wall.
- Position the camera to your desired angle.

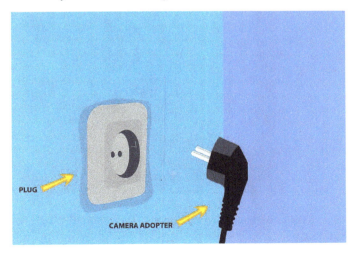

3. Attach your camera to a power source. Almost all cameras come with a power adapter that plugs into a normal wall socket. Plug the small, round end into the power input on the back of the camera and plug the other end into the outlet.

- If your power adapter is missing or broken, contact your manufacturer.

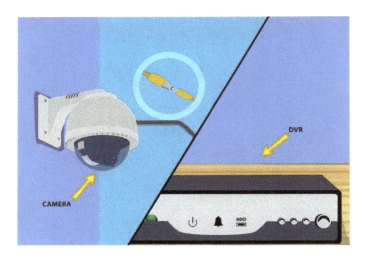

4. Attach a wired camera to your DVR. Surveillance equipment is connected using a BNC (Bayonet Neill–Concelman) connection. BNC cables are simple to use -- they are identical on both sides and you simply plug them into the appropriate port, turning a small nut on the end to lock it in place. Plug one end into your camera's "Output" and the other into one of the DVR "Input" ports.

- Note which input you plug into -- this is the input your DVR must be set to in order to view your camera's video.

- If your cable does not have a BNC connection you can buy a simple BNC adapter online or at a hardware store. This will slip onto the end of your cable to make it BNC compatible.

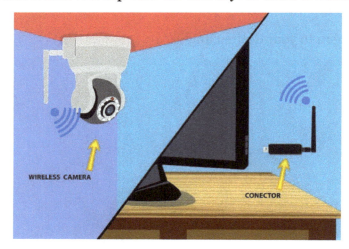

5. Link wireless cameras to your computer. Wireless cameras will come with a software disc that you need to install to view your feeds. Follow the on-screen instructions to access your cameras.

- Some cameras have a small receiver that attaches to your computer through a USB port. Make sure this is properly attached.

- Write down your camera's IP address (ex. 192.168.0.5) if provided -- this number can be typed into any web browser to view your camera remotely.

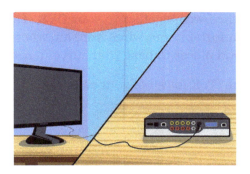

6. Attach the monitor to the DVR. This connection frequently uses a BNC cable as well, but some DVR's can attach with HDMI cables or coaxial cables. Using your preferred connection, attach one end to the DVR's "Output" port and the other to the monitor's "Input."

- You can hook up as many cameras as your DVR has inputs -- it will automatically record every camera you install.

- Note which input you plug into-- this is the input you need to choose to see your cameras.

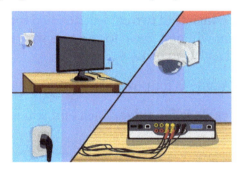

7. Troubleshoot any connection issues. Check that the camera, DVR, and monitor are all hooked up to a power supply and turned on. Make sure your cables are securely attached and that you have selected the right inputs for your DVR and monitor. Some monitors will display every camera at the same time, others have "input" buttons that allow you to switch between cameras.

Method 3

Consolidating your Surveillance System

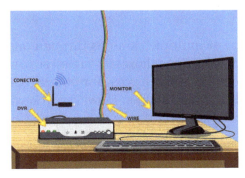

1. Create a central "surveillance hub." When you are wiring a lot of cameras at once, you'll need

one simple place to bring all of the feeds together to your DVR. This should be a place that is easy to access, and where you can comfortably run wires from anywhere in the hotel. Attics, offices and your internet router all make good places to base your surveillance system.

- You should only need one DVR for all of your cameras.

2. Use Siamese cables to wire your system effectively. The most common surveillance cable is a Siamese cable, named because it consists of two cables attached together. One is for power, and the other is for video. This means you will only have to run one wire through the hotel to set up each camera. The cable is usually sold as RG59 or RG6.

- The braided red and black side is for power. Red is positive and black is negative.

- The singular, cylindrical cable is for video. Each end will have either a BNC attachment or a coaxial cable.

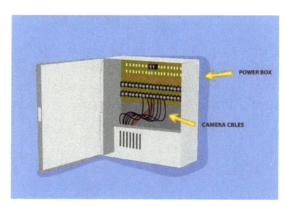

3. Use a power supply box to power multiple cameras through one outlet. Power boxes, available online and in hardware stores for $30-$50, allow you to power your cameras through a single wall outlet. They come with multiple ports and are great for powering close-together cameras or cameras that aren't near an outlet, like attic cameras. However, you will need to run lengthy amounts of wire to attach each camera to the same box.

- Always attach the cameras before hooking the box to electricity.

- Make sure you buy a power supply box big enough to power each one of your cameras. They should list how many outlets they support on the box.

Security Operations in Hotel | 237

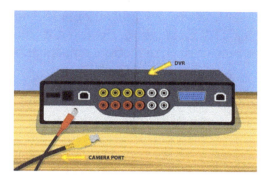

4. Attach each video cable to a separate DVR port. Your DVR can handle multiple cameras at once, allowing you to record every room in the hotel with only one box. Your monitor will then display every camera, or you will have to cycle through them using the "input" button on your DVR.

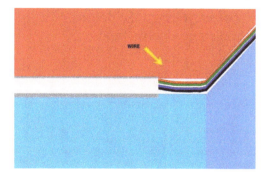

5. Hide your wires. To have a truly professional looking system you can run your cables through the walls and towards your surveillance hub. Be sure you know the layout of your walls and the location of any pipes, cables, or studs as you begin running wires. Running cables requires you to drill a hole in the wall, then thread the cable through the walls to your DVR through open spaces in the hotel, usually the attic.

- If you are not comfortable drilling into your walls and running cables through, call a professional carpenter or handyman to take care of the cabling.

- You can also secure cables to the walls or baseboards using a staple gun.

- Consider hiding cables under rugs, but tape them down so that no one accidentally trips.

6. Alternatively, call security specialists to set up a custom system. There are many security com-

panies that will install cameras, motion sensors, and automatic emergency calling for you, though they cost much more than a typical DIY installation. However, if you have a large hotel, are uncomfortable with wiring, or want extra features like motion-sensors and alarm systems, call a security firm near you.

- ADT, LifeShield, Vivint, and SafeShield are larger, nationwide providers of security systems.

How to Replace a Smoke Detector

Functioning smoke detectors are extremely important in maintaining the safety of the hotel. Smoke detectors need to be replaced every 10 years, and smoke detector batteries should be replaced every 6 months. You may need to replace your smoke detector The process takes just a few minutes and only requires a screwdriver and some electric tape.

Part 1

Identifying Smoke Detectors for Replacement

1. Locate all of your smoke detectors. There should be at least one detector on every floor of the house, including finished attics or basements. You may even have multiple smoke detectors on each floor, so make sure to check every room.

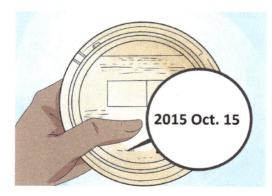

2. Check the manufacture date. The location of the manufacture date should be easy to find but

varies by model. If you find a smoke detector that is over 10 years old, you should replace it immediately. If you can't find a manufacture date on the smoke detector, the detector is probably over 10 years old and should be replaced.

3. Test your smoke detectors. Find the button on the face of the detector and hold it for at least 5 seconds. If the smoke detector beeps, it is functioning properly. If the detector does not beep, something is wrong.

- You may hear all of your smoke alarms beep while only testing one of them; this is normal, and indicates the smoke detector in question is functioning properly.

- You can buy an aerosol can of smoke to test your detector if you wish.

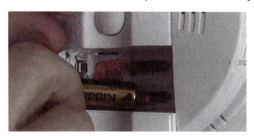

4. Check the batteries on malfunctioning units. Some smoke detectors have batteries, which should be replaced twice a year. If a unit is making a chirping sound, the batteries need replacing. Replace the batteries in the units you've identified as malfunctioning and re-test them. Remember that smoke detectors should be replaced every 10 years, even if replacing the batteries fixes them temporarily. To replace the batteries:

- Remove the detector from the mounting. Most smoke detectors simply require a quarter turn counterclockwise. The detector should now only be attached to a few wires coming out of the ceiling or wall.

- Replace the batteries. Most smoke detectors use 9V batteries. The battery compartment should be visible on the back side of the detector, remove the cover and replace the battery.

- Reattach the detector. Replace the battery cover and hold the smoke detector up against the mounting. Turning the detector clockwise should reattach it to the mount.

- Re-test your detector. Hold the test button for at least 5 seconds. If you hear a beep, your smoke detector is functioning properly.

5. Purchase new smoke detectors. You can purchase smoke detectors online and at most department stores and hardware stores. Deciding on a smoke detector is mostly personal preference, but there are some features to know about.

- Some newer smoke detectors also function as a carbon monoxide detector. If you don't have a CO detector in your house, this is a good option. It is only necessary if you use gas in the house.
- Wireless smoke detectors are convenient, but they can only connect to other wireless alarms of the same model. If you're replacing all of the smoke detectors in your house and choose the wireless option, make sure to purchase the same make and model.
- Check the manufacture date. Since smoke alarms have a fairly static 10-year lifetime, buying one that has been on the shelf for two years will only give you 8 years of use.

Part 2

Removing the Malfunctioning unit

1. Shut off electricity to the detector. To do this, you'll need to find your circuit breaker and switch off power to the smoke detector in question. This will remove the danger of electric shock resulting from touching open wires.

Security Operations in Hotel | 241

2. Remove the old detector from the mounting. Usually this will just involve a quarter turn counterclockwise. The unit will now be suspended from the ceiling by three wires, all connected to the detector via one plug called the wiring harness. These wires are:

- Black - 120 volts

- White - Neutral

- Red or Yellow - Interconnect: This is the wire that connects the alarm with the remaining alarms in your residence.

3. Unhook the wires from the detector. Squeeze both sides of the plastic plug while pulling the plug away from the detector. The old detector should now be completely detached.

4. Remove the mounting plate. Take a screwdriver and remove the two screws that hold the mounting plate to the electrical box in your ceiling. Be careful not to accidentally pull the wires out of the ceiling while removing the mounting plate.

- It's always worth checking to see if the existing mounting plate will work with your new unit before you replace it.

5. Remove the wiring harness. Start by removing any electric tape or wire caps that are attached to the wiring harness. Untwist the wires and remove the wiring harness. The three wires in the ceiling should now just be exposed metal ends.

Part 3
Installing the New Detector

1. Ensure the power is off. If you haven't done so already, make sure to turn the appropriate circuit breaker to the "off" position.

2. Attach the new wiring harness. The new smoke detector should also come with a wiring harness very similar to the one you removed. Match the wires and attach them by twisting the metal ends around each other. Wrap the newly attached metal ends in electric tape or attach a wire cap. Attach the wires in the following manner: black to black, white to white, and red or yellow to the color of the third wire in your ceiling (this color can vary).

   - After attaching the wires, pull down slightly on the wire harness to make sure you have a good connection that can support the weight of the alarm. If the wire harness comes undone you will need to reattach the wires, making sure to wrap them tightly around each other.
   - If there are only two wires, you may only need to attach black to black and white to white.

3. Attach the new mounting plate. Take the new mounting plate that came with the new alarm and pass the wiring harness through the large hole in the center of the plate. Then screw the plate into the ceiling/wall with the two screws that you removed earlier.

4. Connect the new smoke detector. Plug the wiring harness into the new detector, and then attach the smoke detector to the mounting plate. This can most likely be done by holding the detector up on the mounting plate and turning the detector clockwise.

- If your smoke detector is battery powered, don't forget to install new batteries before you attach it to the mounting plate.

5. Turn on the electricity. When you switch the circuit breaker back on, you may hear a beep from your newly installed smoke detector.

6. Test your new smoke detector. All smoke detectors have a "test" button, sometimes it is the only button on the face of the detector. Press and hold the button for at least 5 seconds, and you should hear a beep.

- If you have other working smoke alarms in the house, they may all beep. This is a sign that you connected your new smoke alarm properly.

- If the smoke detector does not beep when tested, check that you matched the wires properly and that they are sufficiently attached at the metal ends. Check the circuit breaker to make sure the power is on.

- You can use an aerosol can of smoke to perform a real test of the detector, if desired.

Permissions

All chapters in this book are published with permission under the Creative Commons Attribution Share Alike License or equivalent. Every chapter published in this book has been scrutinized by our experts. Their significance has been extensively debated. The topics covered herein carry significant information for a comprehensive understanding. They may even be implemented as practical applications or may be referred to as a beginning point for further studies.

We would like to thank the editorial team for lending their expertise to make the book truly unique. They have played a crucial role in the development of this book. Without their invaluable contributions this book wouldn't have been possible. They have made vital efforts to compile up to date information on the varied aspects of this subject to make this book a valuable addition to the collection of many professionals and students.

This book was conceptualized with the vision of imparting up-to-date and integrated information in this field. To ensure the same, a matchless editorial board was set up. Every individual on the board went through rigorous rounds of assessment to prove their worth. After which they invested a large part of their time researching and compiling the most relevant data for our readers.

The editorial board has been involved in producing this book since its inception. They have spent rigorous hours researching and exploring the diverse topics which have resulted in the successful publishing of this book. They have passed on their knowledge of decades through this book. To expedite this challenging task, the publisher supported the team at every step. A small team of assistant editors was also appointed to further simplify the editing procedure and attain best results for the readers.

Apart from the editorial board, the designing team has also invested a significant amount of their time in understanding the subject and creating the most relevant covers. They scrutinized every image to scout for the most suitable representation of the subject and create an appropriate cover for the book.

The publishing team has been an ardent support to the editorial, designing and production team. Their endless efforts to recruit the best for this project, has resulted in the accomplishment of this book. They are a veteran in the field of academics and their pool of knowledge is as vast as their experience in printing. Their expertise and guidance has proved useful at every step. Their uncompromising quality standards have made this book an exceptional effort. Their encouragement from time to time has been an inspiration for everyone.

The publisher and the editorial board hope that this book will prove to be a valuable piece of knowledge for students, practitioners and scholars across the globe.

Index

A
Angry Customers, 53, 56
Apology, 58, 62, 76, 82-83, 85
Appreciation, 34, 78, 89, 91
Armoire, 98
Artificial Light, 100
Automatic Response System, 112

B
Bad Customer, 45, 48
Bathroom Rug, 102
Bleach Soak, 130
Body Language, 15, 67, 111
Break-ins, 17
Budget, 37, 93-94, 98, 101
Business Traveler, 93

C
Calcium Hardness, 181-182, 189, 191, 204, 216
Call Center, 4
Can-do Attitude, 48
Cancellations, 3
Chlorine Shock Product, 202
Clean Bedding, 102-103
Company Merchandise, 114
Complaint-resolution Data, 79
Custom Signature, 36
Customer Database, 86
Customer Interaction, 78
Customer Service Experience, 4, 75
Customer Service Survey, 78, 117
Customer Support, 40-42
Customer Traffic, 72
Customer's Behavior, 58-59
Customer's Grievance, 68
Customer's Language, 75
Customers' Needs, 86

D
Delivery Personnel, 10
Diagonal Views, 96
Digital, 40, 230-232
Discount On Price, 77
Dishwasher, 128-129, 176-177
Dress Code, 13, 39

E
Effective Communicator, 32
Email Language, 31
Employee Performance, 113
Employee Training Program, 110

F
Facebook, 89, 123
Featherbed, 98
Feedback, 28, 45, 57, 77, 86-87, 89-90, 94, 109, 114-118, 123
Financial Report, 35
Food Service, 123-124, 126
Front Desk, 2, 4, 6, 13, 15, 18

G
Gift Cards, 91

H
Hdmi, 98, 235
Hotel Business, 19
Hotel Management, 4, 39, 226
Hotel Policies, 39
Hotel Receptionist, 2-6, 19
Hotel Room, 93-100, 132

I
Industrial Freezer, 124
Infrared Illuminators, 228
Instagram, 123
Interactive Voice Response (IVR) System, 121
Internet, 40-41, 123, 232, 236
Irate Customer, 47, 60, 63-64

L
Laundry Room, 132-135
Loyal Customers, 91

M
Microsoft Office, 5

Mini-fridge, 100

N
Negotiating Skills, 3
Net Promoter Score, 118
Newsletter, 88

O
Outdoor Fountain, 224-225

P
Personal Service, 92
Phone Support, 41-42
Physically Aggressive, 66, 72
Pillow Cases, 103, 107
Point of Sale (POS) System, 122
Polite Phrases, 22, 62
Polls, 87
Pool Skimmer, 187, 203
Problem-solving, 114, 120
Professional Website, 122
Proofreading, 31
Public Health, 94

Q
Quality Control Department, 110
Questionnaires, 87

R
Recurring Problem Customer, 48
Refund, 56, 63, 77, 115

S
Safety Codes, 94
Safety Measures, 17
Service Quality Goals, 113

Service Training, 110
Social Media, 30, 36, 89, 92, 121, 123
Soda Ash, 195-199
Soundproofing, 97-98
Storage Space, 98, 134
Store Credit, 77
Stressful Situations, 3, 16, 59
Surveillance System, 229, 231, 235-236
Surveys, 87, 118

T
Temper, 58-59, 66, 70
Thermoplastics, 226
Threatening, 13, 54, 70, 72
Total Alkalinity, 180-182, 202
Twitter, 89, 123

U
Unsatisfactory Product, 63

V
Vacuum Cleaner, 159-160, 163, 168
Video Recorder (DVR), 231
Vinegar Solution, 128-130, 178
Vinyl Floors, 97
Vision Statement, 120

W
Wi-Fi, 99
Workplace Emails, 33

CPSIA information can be obtained
at www.ICGtesting.com
Printed in the USA
BVHW010237031022
648382BV00049B/674